Raised in Auckland, New Zealand, Kelly Gibney has an obsessive curiosity about food which has taken her overseas to New York and Melbourne. Returning home to inspire others to get into the kitchen and explore great ways of preparing simple and delicious home-cooked meals, she now works as a food writer, stylist and photographer, and has been featured on Radio NZ and TVNZ. Her twin passions for cooking and eating have resulted in an honest, flavour-first approach to wholefoods.

Kelly can be found crafting new recipes in the kitchen, disappearing into the wilderness with her partner, her daughter, and a delightful picnic, as well as between the pages of this book.

CONTENTS

4

INTRODUCTION

Health and food are more intertwined than ever. This is a wonderful thing.

I want to be part of a wave of growing, cooking and eating that releases people from any guilt and deprivation around food and instead delivers delicious, wholesome food that forgets the rules. We are all different. What I need from my diet is probably different than what you need. To avoid the conflicting dietary information, my one piece of advice is to embrace eating mindfully. Slow down, chew every mouthful, and appreciate and notice how you feel after you eat. Let your body guide you and your intuition serve you.

The wellness movement can feel overwhelming, at times. I'm encouraging you to forget about diets and just learn to cook a few more recipes with quality ingredients. You'll be amazed how much your body will love you when you simplify the rules and decide just to relish eating real food. It's okay to be obsessed with food - I definitely am - but only if it's bringing you joy.

I've said in interviews a couple of times that given the choice between sitting at a table with wellbeing experts or chefs, I'd rather be seated with the chefs - I want to find myself where food is celebrated and enjoyed wholeheartedly.

Our relationship with food can be so good. It can bring us nothing but pleasure, and that enjoyment of good food can trickle down to the rest of your family. My daughter Bonnie was an incredibly fussy kid. Our approach

has been to not stress out about it too much – to make sure her experiences around food and eating are free from pressure. We don't make a big deal out of sweet treats, and vegetables are not portrayed as something to be endured. She sees us prepare and enjoy a wide variety of foods, and I think that's key. She wants to be part of what her parents are doing, and this motivates a little bravery on her part to try new foods. She'll now ask to sample things from my plate that she has adamantly refused in the past.

There will always be exceptions, but on the whole, I think parents can afford to worry about this a lot less.

I can't tell you how much it means to me that you've picked up my book. This has been a labour of love, and I hope that cooking and eating from it brings joy to your kitchen.

If you try any of these dishes, please find me on social media and let me know. I adore hearing from readers and peeking at what they've been crafting in their home kitchens.

Much love,

Kelly Gibney

PANTRY AND KITCHEN ESSENTIALS

Here you'll find the ingredients I always have on hand in my kitchen. I've tried to keep these relatively easy to source. They will all be available at supermarkets, health food stores or at good green grocers. I have kept my selection of flours to just a handful, too. I don't want you to have to head to the store with a mile-long list every time you'd like to try a new recipe. When it comes to building up a supply of more expensive ingredients, like cacao powder or quinoa flakes, consider buying a new ingredient every week or two while you stock up your wholefood pantry.

FLOURS

Almond meal / ground almonds
Made by grinding almonds into fine flour, almond meal gives gluten-free baking a moist and delicate crumb. It features heavily in paleo and grain-free recipes. Most of the time, I use an almond meal made with almonds that have had the skins removed, as it produces a softer result in cake and loaf recipes. Sometimes, I'll make my own almond meal in a high-speed blender using whole raw almonds, as I enjoy the coarser result in muesli bars and cookies.

Brown rice flour
You'll find brown rice flour in many of my baking recipes. Sometimes using only almond meal can result in a flavour that is too intense and a texture that is too soft. Brown rice flour adds a nice density and weight. Other than pancakes or pikelets, it can't often be used alone. I combine it with one or two other gluten-free flours (such as buckwheat flour and tapioca flour) to provide the characteristics necessary for a successful flour blend.

Buckwheat flour
This nutritious flour is great when included in a blend with other flours. I'll often pair it with brown rice flour and tapioca flour as my go-to gluten-free blend. I almost never use it alone as its earthy and slightly grassy flavour can be quite strong in large amounts. It also lacks the structure to be the sole flour in most recipes. Buckwheat crepes are the one exception to this rule. The flavour of buckwheat is delicious in this wafer-thin form. Buy in small quantities to ensure freshness. Can be stored in the fridge.

Tapioca flour
Tapioca flour is awesome. Made from the roots of the cassava plant, it finds a home in paleo and grain-free recipes as it has a wonderful starchy quality and is not made from a grain. Not often used alone outside of the paleo realm, it can be blended with brown rice flour and almond meal (or buckwheat flour) to create a successful gluten-free baking blend, and is a great binder for fritters or burger patties. It is responsible for the crispiness of my peanut butter cookies. I love to dust it over fresh fish before pan-frying.

White rice flour
I don't use white rice flour as often as the other flours, but it is an essential ingredient in my gluten-free, sweet potato gnocchi. Its sticky and glutinous nature makes it ideal for binding. You can use it to bind fritters or pancakes, and it's great for coating fresh fish before frying. Not often used in baking, white rice flour cannot be interchanged with brown rice flour as they have very different qualities.

6

Quinoa flakes

Quinoa flakes can be used in many of the places you might traditionally use rolled oats. They won't absorb quite as much liquid as oats, so you may need to reduce the liquid component slightly if adapting an oat recipe. I love quinoa flakes in crumble toppings and in cookies. It has the subtle grassy flavour of quinoa and is lovely in buttery or vanilla-based recipes.

SWEETENERS

The world of natural sweeteners can be incredibly confusing. People are often happy to use large handfuls of dates, but scared to explore unrefined sugars like rapadura or muscovado. Here's my take: it's ALL essentially sugar and should be enjoyed with a very light touch. I keep well away from the processed white stuff, but enjoy exploring all the choices in the world of unrefined and lightly refined sweeteners. In baking, liquid sweeteners like honey and maple syrup will give a more fudgy result, while granular sweeteners (like coconut sugar) give a more defined crumb. Rather than sticking to just one sweetener for everything, appreciate
the different ways each can complement your cooking.

Pure maple syrup

The stuff of gods. Porridge and pancakes just scream out to be drizzled in this amber goodness. Make sure you get a maple syrup that is 100% pure. Cheaper varieties will often contain some sneaky sugar. Pure maple syrup is quite pricey but adds incredible flavour. I love using it in my cooking and baking.

Rice malt syrup

I always have some of this on hand. Though it is rather processed, I like the gentle sweetness. Free from fructose, it's a great choice for those who are sensitive to this type of sugar. You'll need to increase the quantity slightly when using it in a recipe that lists maple syrup or honey, as it is much less sweet. It is significantly cheaper than pure maple syrup so can be a good pantry staple.

Coconut sugar

Coconut sugar has a lovely caramel flavour and stands in for table sugar perfectly when stirring into coffee or sprinkling over porridge. I use coconut sugar and light muscovado sugar interchangeably.

Light muscavado sugar

This is another sugar I always have on hand. Its light caramel flavour and small granules mean it's a great all-purpose sweetener. It's widely available and relatively inexpensive.

Dates

Dates add a richness and stickiness that is wonderful in raw desserts and in fudgy chocolate cakes or brownies. I use them to bind the crust in my Chocolate and Rosemary Tart (see page 178) and as the sweetener in my Perfect Coconut Porridge (see page 18). In baking, I use dried dates (available from the supermarket) that I've soaked in boiling water for 10 minutes. In raw treats or to stir through Middle Eastern pilafs, I will splurge on gorgeous medjool dates. These are wonderful stuffed with almond butter, too.

Honey

Nothing beats the incredible flavour of good-quality honey. I love the distinct flavours of the different varieties available. My family and I have a small spoonful of manuka honey most days for its health benefits. I use honey lightly in cooking and baking as it has a strong and distinctive flavour so should only be used when suitable. Root vegetables are divine when roasted with a drizzle over the top, goat cheese is incredible with honeycomb and there is nothing lovelier for afternoon tea than a moist, honey-sweetened, flourless lemon cake. Cooking destroys many of the beneficial properties of honey so save your pure manuka honey for ingesting raw and use a less expensive honey for cooking.

FATS

Don't be afraid to use healthy fats liberally in your cooking. Fat nourishes our brains and helps our body absorb fat-soluble vitamins. Steer clear of processed fats like soy, canola, corn oil or anything simply labeled 'vegetable oil'. These degrade easily when heated, becoming toxic. They will hurt rather than nourish your body. Switching to fats that your body recognizes, that are stable when heated and that were not created in a lab will be a big step towards good health.

Ghee

All hail ghee. This is hands-down my favourite cooking oil. Its gorgeous golden colour looks so pretty sitting on my kitchen bench. Ghee is essentially clarified butter that has been heated over a long period of time. The milk solids become lightly toasted and separate before drifting to the bottom of the pot. The liquid is then strained, leaving pure butterfat. Those who do not tolerate dairy very well can often still use ghee because of the absence of milk solids. Unlike butter, it will handle a lot of heat without burning. I use it as my everyday oil. If I need to roast some vegetables, I melt the necessary amount and toss through as I would any other oil. It adds an incredible flavour.

Butter

We are liberal users of butter in my household. I'm so happy that research coming out now supports bringing fat back into our diets. It means that people can enjoy this delicious food without guilt. Nothing beats butter on freshly made bread and scones or tossed through steamed vegetables. Butter adds the divine richness to pastries and the golden crispness to crumbles. I often stir a spoonful through cooked millet or rice before serving it to my daughter — she adores it.

Coconut oil

The huge surge in the popularity of all things coconut means coconut oil is very widely available now. After ghee, it is the cooking oil I use most often. However, it's really important to match its distinctive flavour to the right dishes. Asian dishes, sautéed vegetables and baking all benefit from cooking with coconut oil. I find egg dishes, meat and roast potatoes all rather odd when cooked with it, though. It helps create a silky texture in raw-food desserts.

Lard / Tallow

Don't be frightened to include lard (pork fat) or tallow (beef fat) in your diet. If you're not a vegetarian, there is no reason not to consider including it in your oil arsenal. As well as taking a waste-free approach and embracing using every available part of the animal, your health will benefit because these fats don't degrade in the body like cheap vegetable oils do. They are also highly heat-stable. This makes them an excellent choice for stir-fries or any shallow frying you might do.

I obtain tallow by using the rendered fat that is left over when I roast beef bones to make bone broth. I also utilise the solid layer of fat that sits on top of my cooled broth once it's been in the fridge. I simmer it for about 10 minutes to remove any water that may linger.

You can also buy ethical lard from good grocery stores.

Olive oil

I love to drizzle olive oil over my salads and through grain dishes. I use it if I'm sautéing at a low temperature or doing slow (and low) cooking in the oven. Olive oil will degrade at moderate to high heat, so select different oil if that's what you need.

I use light olive oil in my homemade mayonnaise, as its subtle flavour works best. Nothing beats dipping a torn chunk of fresh sourdough into good-quality, extra virgin olive oil.

OTHERS FAVOURITE INGREDIENTS

Raw cacao powder

Though it looks identical to regular dark cocoa powder, raw cacao powder boasts a wealth of antioxidants and minerals that its more processed counterpart does not. Chocolate can be a truly wholesome treat with this superfood included. I love using it in warming drinks, raw chocolate, smoothies and raw treats. It is a rather pricey ingredient, but worth it.

Sweet potato

In New Zealand, sweet potatoes are known as orange kumara. I've used the term "sweet potato" rather than "orange kumara", as it is generic and widely-known. If you have access to the other varieties of kumara (purple and gold), you can swap the orange kumara in my recipes for gold but not purple kumara, as its starch levels and texture are quite different.

Salt
I love salt and I'm not afraid to use it liberally if it is good-quality. I use pink Himalayan mineral salt and flaky New Zealand sea salt in my cooking and on our table. I avoid common table salt and commercial iodised salt as these lack the healthy minerals contained in the other varieties.

KITCHEN TOOLS

Having the right tools on hand makes a huge difference in your enjoyment of cooking and the speed with which you can whip up meals. Of course, budget comes into play when you are starting to add to your kitchen set up, so I've outlined my favourite tools at both ends of the price scale.

Food processor
I consider a food processor pretty darned essential. I use mine constantly for pesto, nut butter, cookies, simple cakes, making nut and oat flour, mayonnaise and lots more. The model I have cost about $300. That outlay vs. how much I have used it makes it very reasonable. Buy one that is as powerful as possible. Mine came with lots of attachments that I've truthfully never really used.

Blender
I have a Vitamix, an incredibly powerful blender that has replaced many other tools in my kitchen. It can make nut butter in minutes, grind nuts into flour, puree whole raw vegetables into wholefood juices, craft velvety smoothies, on top of generally just kicking ass at every task you throw its way. These are pretty expensive machines but worth the investment if you are health- and kitchen-obsessed like me.

If a high-speed blender is out of your price range, an ordinary blender will still be great if you're looking to support your smoothie habit. Make sure you get a model that is able to blitz up greens beautifully. Avoid one with a jug that is too large as these can struggle to blitz ice.

Hand blender
I love my hand blender. It's great for pureeing soups in the pot, blitzing together creamy dressings and making small amounts of hummus.

Mandoline
Owning a mandoline will help you create beautiful wafer-thin vegetable slices that turn your salads into works of art. A mandoline is essential for creating the sweet potato chips for my vegan nachos and the layers in my paleo lasagna. They are also a lifesaver when making big batches of sauerkraut. You can chop large quantities of cabbage in no time at all. There is no need to buy an expensive chefs' version. You can purchase good-quality (inexpensive) hand-held mandolines at good kitchen stores.

Julienne peeler
I'm a big fan of this handy kitchen tool. It'll have you making gorgeous slaws like a pro, and your stir-fries will come together in mere minutes. Just like the mandoline, it is possible to buy inexpensive hand-held varieties.

Spiraliser
The modern wave of interest in wellness and healthy eating has brought with it the spiraliser. Easily turn vegetables into gorgeous noodles that can replace the conventional variety in your favourite pasta and noodle dishes. Being able to make zucchini noodles at home will open up a whole new realm of delicious wholefood dishes. Spiralisers vary wildly in price and also in quality, so ask around and buy one that has been tried and loved by friends.

9

	serving units		vegetarian (VEG)
	dairy free (DF)		nut free (NF)
	gluten free (GF)		grain free (GRFR)
	vegan (VEGN)		

BRUNCH

Sweet potato & kale waffles w/ avocado & pea cream	12 — GF VEG GRFR
Indian spiced brown rice pudding	14 — DF GF NF VEGN
Bolognese omelette	16 — DF GF NF GRFR
Crispy kale omelette	16 — DF GF VEG NF GRFR
Perfect coconut porridge w/ buckwheat & oats	18 — DF NF VEGN
Magical immunity smoothie	20 — DF GF GRFR VEGN
Zinc boost smoothie	20 — DF GF GRFR VEGN
Cauliflower rice kedgeree	22 — DF GF NF GRFR
Brunch loaf w/ sundried tomatoes, olives & basil	24 — GF VEG GRFR
My favourite muffins w/ apple, coconut & banana	26 — DF GF VEG GRFR
Breakfast slice w/ salmon, peas & dill	28 — GF GRFR
Turmeric latte w/ cinnamon & black pepper	30 — DF GF GRFR VEGN
Strawberry & thyme thick shake	30 — DF GF GRFR VEGN
Orange, ginger & cacao no-grain-ola	32 — DF GF GRFR VEGN
Spiced pumpkin pancakes	34 — DF GF VEG GRFR
Buckwheat crepes w/ silky scrambled eggs & smoked salmon	36 — GF NF
Breakfast cookies	38 — DF GF GRFR VEGN
Baked oatmeal w/ banana & nutmeg	40 — DF VEG NF
Breakfast salad	42 — GF VEG NF GRFR

SWEET POTATO & KALE WAFFLES
w/ avocado & pea Cream

Something about the shape of waffles makes them totally irresistible to me.
I like the sweet variety, but I love using savoury flavours even more. Waffles
can be prepared up to a day in advance and gently reheated in the oven
when you're ready to use them. I often make a double batch and freeze
some to pull out when I want to throw a breakfast or supper together quickly.

12

1 cup (210g) cooked sweet potato flesh* –
mashed with a fork
¾ cup (90g) tapioca flour
¾ cup (85g) almond meal
3 free-range eggs – lightly beaten
1 cup (120g) finely grated parmesan
¼ brown onion – finely diced
Large handful kale – cut into very fine ribbons

PEA & AVOCADO CREAM
½ cup (80g) peas
1 ripe avocado
1 small garlic clove – finely diced
Juice of 1 lime
Salt and cracked black pepper

TO SERVE
250g cherry tomatoes – halved / quartered
Fresh basil leaves

*The best way to obtain the kumara flesh is to bake
1–2 medium or large kumara in their skin in the oven
at 180°C (350°F) for approximately one hour until
very tender. Cut in half lengthways and scoop out.
Mash well (using no butter or milk) and cool completely
before using in this recipe.*

Use a blender, hand blender or small food processor to blitz the avocado and pea cream ingredients until smooth. Taste and season well.

Combine all waffle ingredients in a large bowl and mix for a few minutes until well combined. This step works very well in a food processor. Season generously with salt and pepper.

Heat the waffle iron and lightly oil. Spoon the mixture until the waffle indent is three quarters full. Cook for 5–10 minutes (depending on size of waffle) until crisp and golden. Keep the finished waffles warm in the oven until you have used all the batter.

To Serve:
Divide hot waffles among the plates. Dollop the avocado and pea cream on top and serve with halved cherry tomatoes. Garnish with fresh basil leaves.

Cooked waffles will last up to three days in the fridge and can be reheated in the oven. Can be frozen successfully for up to a month.

13

INDIAN SPICED BROWN RICE PUDDING

This version of rice pudding embraces warming Indian spices and makes use of leftover brown rice – I love the firm bite of this whole grain. You can use white rice instead if that's what you have handy, also millet or quinoa.

I prefer a light sweetness, so you may want to add extra sugar if you have a sweet tooth.

14

1 cup (200g) **cooked brown rice**
1½ cups (375ml) **coconut milk** (or coconut cream for extra richness)
½ teaspoon **vanilla paste**
or 1 teaspoon good-quality **vanilla essence**
½ teaspoon **ground cardamom**
Pinch **cinnamon**
Pinch **nutmeg**
Pinch **saffron threads** – lightly crushed
1 rounded tablespoon **coconut sugar**
or **light muscavado sugar**
Small grind of **cracked black pepper**

Combine all the ingredients in a medium saucepan. Simmer 20–25 minutes until thick and creamy. Garnish with fresh fruit, chopped nuts and a drizzle of coconut cream or yoghurt.

BOLOGNESE OMELETTE

You might be thinking I'm a little crazy with this recipe but trust me – it's SO good. A deliciously rich and savoury brunch dish that will fill you up for the rest of the day. Perfect if you've got some of my Ultimate Bolognese left over. I like to cook this over a reasonably high heat to get some good colour and caramelisation on the meat pieces that poke through the egg. Give it a go! Wonderful paired with some avocado, greens and sauerkraut.

3 large free-range **eggs** – lightly beaten
½ cup (115g) leftover **Bolognese sauce**
(see page 110)
Ghee (see page 198) **/ other oil**
Salt and **cracked black pepper**

TO SERVE
Shaved parmesan (optional)
Cracked black pepper

Beat eggs and a pinch of salt together lightly. Gently mix in the Bolognese sauce without breaking up all the chunks.

Heat a generous spoonful of ghee or oil in a sauté pan over a medium-high heat. Add egg and cook for 2 minutes until golden brown on the bottom. Fold in half and cook for a further 2 minutes until set in the middle.

Top with shaved parmesan, if using, and a good grind of cracked black pepper. Serve immediately.

16

CRISPY KALE OMELETTE

This incredibly simple omelette really shines when you're able to get the edges of the kale nice and crisp (think kale chips). Make sure the pan is really hot before you sauté the kale. I've kept this dairy free but a handful of finely grated parmesan or cheddar would be great if you are so inclined.

4 large **kale leaves** – stems removed
and torn into large pieces
3 free-range **eggs** – lightly beaten
Salt and **cracked black pepper**
Ghee (see page 198) **/ coconut oil** for frying

TO GARNISH
Pumpkin seeds

Heat two generous spoonfuls of oil over a medium or high heat. Add the kale and sauté for 3–4 minutes until softened and edges crispy. Season well. Remove from pan and set aside.

Reduce heat to medium and add a little more ghee or oil to the pan if necessary. Pour in the eggs. Allow to set on the bottom of the pan for 1 minute before scattering the kale over the top. When the inside is mostly set, fold the omelette in half and remove from heat. Serve immediately.

PERFECT COCONUT PORRIDGE
w/ buckwheat & oats

This is the beautifully warming breakfast our family eats when the weather chills. Soak the oats and buckwheat overnight to help them become more easily digestible. The oats add a lovely creaminess that balances out the earthy flavor of buckwheat.

Keep toppings simple or customise them as my four-year-old daughter Bonnie likes to. Her breakfast normally includes a drizzle of almond butter, fresh berries, bee pollen – and whatever else takes her fancy. Put some options out and let little (and big) people get creative!

18

½ cup (95g) **raw buckwheat groats**
½ cup (50g) **oats**
6–8 **dried dates** (depending on preferred sweetness), finely chopped
2 cups (500ml) **water**
1 cup (250ml) **coconut cream**
1 teaspoon good-quality **vanilla essence**
Pinch **salt**

Place the oats and buckwheat in two large bowls (each in a separate bowl) and cover with cold water. Soak for 8–12 hours. Drain and rinse well using a sieve.

Place in a medium saucepan along with the other ingredients. Bring to a boil before reducing to a simmer and gently cooking for 25 minutes. Stir regularly as the porridge can stick to the bottom of the pan. Add additional coconut cream or water if the pot becomes too dry.

Porridge is ready when the buckwheat is tender and the consistency is creamy.

Leftover porridge can be gently reheated in a saucepan with a lid on. Add a little more coconut cream, if needed, to loosen.

19

If the porridge clings to the bottom of the pan while cooking, remove the saucepan from the heat and place a lid on top. Leave for 2 minutes. The steam will loosen the porridge and you'll be able to stir it again before placing it on the heat to finish cooking.

MAGICAL IMMUNITY SMOOTHIE

This smoothie always makes me feel SO much better when I'm unwell or coming down with something. The combination of ingredients is bright and sunny with a big hit of goodness. Healing turmeric is more easily absorbed with the help of a little black pepper. Go ahead and enjoy this drink even when you're not sick. It's a lovely accompaniment to shared brunches. You'll need a powerful, high-speed blender to break down the carrots to a silky-smooth consistency.

1 **orange** – peel removed
2 medium **carrots** – trimmed, peeled and cut into chunks
1 **mango** – peeled, stone removed and cut into chunks
½ teaspoon **ground turmeric**
Grind of **cracked black pepper**
1¾ cups (180ml) **almond milk** or **any non-dairy milk**
2 handfuls **ice**

Combine all ingredients in a high-speed blender. Blitz until smooth and velvety. Add a little extra almond milk or water if a thinner consistency is preferred. Serve immediately.

🍶 2   Ⓐ DF   🌱 GF   🌿 GRFR   🌱 VEGN

ZINC BOOST SMOOTHIE

A big dose of plant-based goodness is a wonderful way to start the day. Get immunity-boosting, skin-loving zinc from the pumpkin seeds, gut-healthy probiotics from the coconut yogurt, and a gentle, creamy sweetness from the frozen banana.

¼ cup (35g) **pumpkin seeds** – soaked overnight in water. Drained and rinsed well
¼ cup (35g) **raw almonds** – soaked overnight in water. Drained and rinsed well
1 **frozen banana** – peeled and cut into large chunks
½ cup (125ml) **coconut yoghurt**
1½ cups (375ml) **almond milk**
Large handful **spinach leaves**
Large handful **ice**

Place all ingredients into a blender (preferably a powerful one) and blitz until creamy and very smooth. Add extra almond milk or water if a thinner consistency is preferred. Serve immediately.

CAULIFLOWER RICE KEDGEREE

My grandparents moved to New Zealand from India in the 1950s. This Anglo-Indian dish is something my mum grew up eating, and she in turn served it to my sister and me. It has always been a family favourite. My version uses cauliflower 'rice' instead of white rice. This means I can eat big, greedy portions without needing a nap afterward! Traditionally it's served at brunch but feel free to serve this up for lunch or dinner.

22

Cut the cauliflower into florets. Blitz in a food processor in 3–4 batches until a rice-like texture is achieved. Be careful not to let it get too fine or the end result will be mushy when cooked.

Place mustard seeds in a dry sauté pan over a medium or low heat. Move around the pan gently for 1–2 minutes until fragrant. Use a mortar and pestle to crush the seeds into a rough powder.

Heat two tablespoons of ghee or coconut oil in a sauté pan over a medium heat. Add the onion, garlic, ginger and chilli. Cook for approximately 5 minutes, without browning, until the onion is translucent and tender. Add the curry powder, mustard seeds and capsicum. Cook for a further minute.

Add two more tablespoons of oil along with the cauliflower rice. Increase the heat to high and move around the pan for 2 minutes. Add the coconut cream and cook, stirring often, for 5–10 minutes until the cauliflower is tender but not mushy.

Break the smoked fish into large chunks and add to the pan along with the parsley. Toss gently through the kedgeree. Season to taste.

Bring a large saucepan of water to a boil. Add the eggs gently and cook for 6 minutes. Remove and run under cold water. Peel gently and cut into halves or quarters.

Lay the eggs on top of the finished kedgeree. Scatter additional fresh parsley leaves and pumpkin seeds on top. Serve immediately.

Will keep for two days in an airtight container in the fridge. Reheat gently in a sauté pan.

1 medium **cauliflower**
1 teaspoon **mustard seeds**
1 **onion** – finely diced
3 large **garlic cloves** – finely diced
1 rounded teaspoon finely **grated ginger**
1 large **red chilli** – seeds removed and finely diced
1 tablespoon **mild curry powder**
1 **capsicum** – seeds removed and cut into 1cm cubes
¾ cup (180ml) **coconut cream**
350g good-quality **smoked fish** – skin and bones removed
Large handful **fresh parsley** – roughly chopped
3 free-range **eggs**
Salt and **cracked black pepper**
4 tablespoons **ghee** (see page 198) or **coconut oil** for sautéing

TO GARNISH
Parsley
Pumpkin seeds
Lemon wedges

23

BRUNCH LOAF
w/ sundried tomatoes, olives & basil

Pair with a pot of coffee and a generous lick of butter for my perfect way to start the day. I love this for shared brunches, my mad on-the-go mornings or alongside some softly scrambled eggs when I need alot of energy for a big day. It's even better the day after baking, so prep the night before if you are serving it up to friends in the morning.

5 **free-range eggs** – lightly beaten
1 **garlic clove** – finely diced
1 rounded teaspoon **gluten-free baking powder**
2¼ cups (250g) **almond moal**
1 cup (135g) grated **sweet potato**
1 cup (100g) grated **cheddar cheese**
or **parmesan**
12 **pitted black olives** – each sliced in 3, across
6 **sundried tomatoes** – cut into ribbons
3 tablespoons **olive oil / melted ghee**
(see page 198)
¾ teaspoon **sea salt**
Cracked black pepper

TO GARNISH
Pumpkin, sunflower and sesame seeds
Additional sliced black olives

Preheat oven to 165°C (329°F).

Mix egg, garlic, almond meal and baking powder in a large bowl. Add the remaining ingredients and stir until well combined.

Grease and line a 23cm loaf pan. Use a spatula to fill the tin with the loaf batter and even out the surface. Sprinkle with seeds and additional olives.

Bake for 50–60 minutes until golden and a skewer comes out clean when inserted.

Let cool for 45 minutes before slicing.

Can be stored in the fridge for up to four days.

MY FAVOURITE MUFFINS
w/ apple, coconut & banana

These simple but lovely muffins really hit the spot for breakfast. They are wholesome enough to enjoy regularly and are wonderful for kids. I add only a teensy bit of maple syrup to sweeten them, but they're great even if you omit it entirely.

Makes 12 muffins

1 very **ripe banana** – lightly mashed
4 free-range **eggs**
1 cup (110g) **almond meal**
1 cup (100g) **desiccated coconut**
¼ cup (30g) **tapioca flour**
2 tablespoons **pure maple syrup**
or **rice malt syrup**
¾ teaspoon **baking soda**
1 teaspoon **apple cider vinegar**
1 teaspoon good-quality **vanilla essence**
2 medium **red apples**

Preheat oven to 180°C (350°F)

Combine all ingredients except apple in a food processor and run until the batter is smooth. Scrape the sides as necessary.

Cut 1½ apples into 1cm cubes. Gently fold this through the batter.

Pour into a well-greased or lined 12-hole muffin tin. Cut the remaining apple into thin slices and place one on top of each muffin.

Bake for 25–35 minutes until golden and a skewer comes out clean when inserted.

Will last up to three days in an airtight container.

BREAKFAST SLICE
w/ salmon, peas & dill

A fabulous option for a shared brunch. No need to cook individual eggs for each person. Ideally use smoked salmon fillets rather than cold-smoked salmon slices. The nut and seed topping adds a yummy crunch. Pair with a green salad, cherry tomatoes and avocado wedges.

28

8 free range **eggs** lightly beaten
½ cup (55g) **almond meal / chickpea flour**
1 cup (135g) grated **sweet potato**
1 cup (120g) finely grated **parmesan / cheddar**
½ cup (80g) **peas** (adding straight from frozen is fine)
Zest of 1 **lemon**
Handful **fresh dill** – roughly chopped
150–200g **smoked salmon fillet**
Salt and **cracked black pepper**
½ cup (70g) **mixed seeds / nuts** to top – I've used pumpkin seeds, pine nuts and sliced almonds

Preheat oven to 200°C (390°F)

Combine eggs, almond meal and sweet potato in a large bowl and mix well. Stir through the remaining ingredients except the salmon.

Pour half of the egg mixture into a lined 25cm square baking dish. Break the salmon into large chunks and scatter over the dish. Pour the rest of the egg over the top. Wiggle the dish slightly on the counter to flatten the surface of the slice. Sprinkle with the nuts and seeds.

Bake for 30–35 minutes until firm and golden. Leave to sit for 15 minutes before slicing.

Leftovers will keep in the fridge in an airtight container for three days.

1 DF GF GRFR VEGN

TURMERIC LATTE
w/ cinnamon & black pepper

I can only drink one small coffee a day, otherwise, I'm just too wired and can't function efficiently. My second hot drink of the day is often a turmeric latte. Though caffeine-free, this drink is energising and deeply warming – not to mention beautiful to look at! The healing properties of turmeric, cinnamon and ginger deliver a heap of goodness in a deliciously spicy way. Black pepper helps your body absorb the turmeric and adds a pleasant zing.

1 cup (250ml) unsweetened almond milk
½ teaspoon ground turmeric
1 teaspoon finely grated, fresh ginger root
Generous pinch ground cinnamon
Grind of cracked black pepper
2 teaspoons good-quality coconut oil
2 teaspoons coconut sugar
or pure maple syrup or raw honey

Heat the almond milk until very hot but not boiling, then place in a blender along with the other ingredients. Blitz until the texture is frothy and the ginger and spices are thoroughly blended.

Serve immediately.

30

2 DF GF GRFR VEGN

STRAWBERRY & THYME THICK SHAKE

Herbs and fruit play beautifully together on an icy creamy base. For breakfast or as a snack, this is a dreamy blend.

1 frozen banana – cut into chunks
1 heaped cup (160g) fresh
or frozen strawberries
1½ cups (375ml) almond / coconut milk
1 teaspoon fresh thyme leaves
1 teaspoon good-quality vanilla essence
Large handful ice

Place all ingredients in a powerful blender and blitz until smooth.

Serve immediately.

ORANGE, GINGER
& cacao no-grain-ola

There are so many ways you can enjoy this tasty grain-free delight. Pair with icy cold milk in the morning, create a parfait with yoghurt and fresh fruit, eat it by the handful as a snack, use it to top poached fruit (lazy crumble!) or place in a lovely large jar and give as a gift.

1 tablespoon **coconut oil** or **melted butter**
or **ghee** (see page 198)
¼ cup (60ml) **pure maple syrup** (if using rice
malt syrup increase to ⅓ cup)
1 tablespoon **cacao powder**
or good-quality **dark cocoa powder**
2 teaspoons good-quality **vanilla essence**
2 pinches **salt**
1 teaspoon **ground ginger**
½ teaspoon **ground cinnamon**
¼ teaspoon **ground nutmeg**
1 cup (115g) **slivered almonds**
1 cup (75g) **unsweetened coconut flakes**
(sometimes called coconut chips)
½ cup (70g) **raw pumpkin seeds**
½ cup (70g) **raw cashew nuts**
½ cup (85g) **raw brazil nuts**
¼ cup (40g) **sesame seeds**
Zest of 1 orange

Preheat oven to 140°C (285°F)

Combine coconut oil, maple syrup, cacao powder, vanilla essence, salt, ginger, cinnamon and nutmeg in a small saucepan over a low heat. Whisk together until the coconut oil is liquid and the mixture is smooth.

Pour over the nuts, seeds and coconut in a large bowl. Toss to coat well.

Spread out evenly on a large baking sheet lined with baking paper.

Bake for 25 minutes, tossing at least once during the cooking process.

Remove from oven, scatter the orange zest and toss well. Leave to cool completely.

Store in an airtight container for up to one week.

SPICED PUMPKIN PANCAKES

Pancakes can be on the menu regularly when you opt to make them with a more wholesome touch. I adore the warm spices and soft pumpkin sweetness in this recipe. Dollop coconut yoghurt (or full-fat Greek yoghurt) with real vanilla bean and a touch of maple syrup or honey atop your stack and serve.

Makes 12 pancakes

¾ cup (175g) **roasted pumpkin flesh***
4 free-range **eggs**
1 teaspoon good-quality **vanilla essence**
¼ cup (60ml) **pure maple syrup**
or **rice malt syrup** (rice malt will be less sweet)
¼ cup (60ml) **almond / coconut milk**
1½ cups (175g) **almond meal**
½ cup (60g) **tapioca flour**
1 teaspoon **gluten-free baking powder**
½ teaspoon **ground cinnamon**
¼ teaspoon **ground nutmeg**
Coconut oil / ghee (see page 198) for frying

* To obtain the roasted pumpkin flesh, cut ¼ of a crown pumpkin into large chunks, toss with melted coconut oil or ghee and roast at 180℃ until very tender. Mash roughly with a fork before pressing tightly into a measuring cup to gain correct amount. Do not boil the pumpkin as it will be too watery.

Combine all ingredients in a food processor and mix until the batter is smooth.

Heat a generous dollop of oil in a large sauté pan over a medium heat. Cook the batter ¼ cup at a time. Use the back of a spoon to flatten the batter a little once it hits the pan. You should be able to fit 2–3 pancakes in the pan at one time. Each side will need about 2 minutes. Flip with care as the batter is delicate. Reduce heat if the pancakes are cooking too quickly.

Store the pancakes in a warm oven until you have used all the batter.

Leftover pancakes can be stored in the fridge for up to two days. Gently reheat in the oven.

34

BUCKWHEAT CREPES
w/ silky scrambled eggs & smoked salmon

I make up batches of buckwheat crepes in advance and freeze them.
It makes a stunning breakfast come together very quickly – even on a
weekday! My instructions for scrambled eggs will ensure you have gorgeously
creamy eggs and a breakfast to rival any fancy café fare.

CREPES
1 cup (145g) **buckwheat flour**
1 cup (250ml) **milk** (dairy or non-dairy will both work)
¼ cup (60ml) **olive oil** / **melted butter**
3 free-range **eggs** – lightly beaten
Ghee (see page 198) / **butter** for sautéing

SCRAMBLE
¼ teaspoon **salt**
8 free-range **eggs** (for scrambling) – lightly beaten
8 slices **cold-smoked salmon** / **gravlax**
3 tablespoons **ghee** / **butter** for cooking

TO SERVE
Finely chopped chives
Avocado slices

To make the crepes:
Whisk the buckwheat flour, milk, oil, eggs and salt together in a large bowl until smooth.

Heat a spoonful of ghee or butter in a sauté or crepe pan over medium heat. Pour ¼ cup of batter into the pan and swirl the pan a little to spread the mixture thinly. Cook for 1 minute before flipping, then cook for a further minute. Watch the temperature of the pan, it shouldn't get too hot. You are aiming for a light golden colour. Repeat until all the batter is used. Add additional ghee or butter as needed. Store crepes, covered, in a warm oven until ready to use, or make up to 24 hours in advance.

Crepes can be reheated gently in a warm sauté pan or in the oven on a low heat.

To make the scamble:
Season the beaten eggs with salt. Heat a large sauté pan over a low heat. Add three tablespoons of ghee or butter and wait until melted and foamy. Add the eggs, leave to sit for 5 seconds and then use a spatula to gently move the eggs around the pan. Use long swirling motions, bringing the eggs from the outside of the pan into the middle. Once the eggs are 80 percent cooked, remove from the heat (they will continue to set).

Place a warm buckwheat crepe on each plate and divide the scrambled egg among them. Add two slices of smoked salmon and sliced avocado (if using) to each and fold crepe over. Garnish with freshly chopped chives.

Serve immediately.

37

BREAKFAST COOKIES

With the goodness of banana, nuts and seeds (and not much sugar), these
are a great little breakfast treat. The outside is pleasingly crisp and the inside
soft and fudgy. In our household, these appear alongside a cup of strong
black coffee for the adults, and clutched in the hands of little ones running
outside to play. I hope they find a home in your weekend morning rituals.

Makes 12-15 cookies

1 ripe banana – roughly mashed
¾ cup (180g) almond butter
1 teaspoon good-quality vanilla essence
3 tablespoons coconut sugar
or light muscavado sugar
1 cup (100g) desiccated coconut
½ cup (70g) raw cashew nuts
¼ cup (35g) raw pumpkin seeds
2–3 tablespoons raw cacao nibs
(can add as desired)

Preheat oven to 180°C (350°F)

Combine all ingredients in a food processor
and run until thoroughly combined. Scrape
the sides as needed. Use damp hands (the
mixture is very sticky!) to form large, heaped
teaspoons of mixture into balls. Place on a
baking sheet lined with baking paper. Use
your fingers or a fork to press them down.

Bake for 15–18 minutes until golden. Leave
on the tray to cool for 30 minutes before
consuming. Cookies will last up to four days
in an airtight container. They freeze well for
up to two months.

BAKED OATMEAL
w/ banana & nutmeg

Breakfast can be simple AND delicious AND feel just that little bit special.
Serve with a drizzle of my coconut custard (see page 190),
yoghurt (dairy or coconut) or, for really delicious indulgence,
some organic cream.

40

2 cups (200g) **rolled oats**
2 free-range **eggs** – lightly beaten
1 **apple** – core removed, grated (skin on)
and with the liquid squeezed out
1 ¼ cups (310ml) **full-fat coconut cream**
or **almond milk**
1 teaspoon good-quality **vanilla extract**
¼ cup (50g) **coconut sugar**
or **light muscavado sugar**,
plus an extra teaspoon for sprinkling
¼ teaspoon **ground nutmeg**
2 **ripe bananas** – sliced into 2mm slices

Preheat oven to 180°C (350°F)

Combine all the ingredients (except banana)
in a large bowl and mix well.

Grease an oven-proof dish really well. I use a
22cm round skillet.

Pour in half the oat mixture. Tile the top of
the batter with half of the bananas. Pour the
remaining batter on top, tiling it with the rest
of the banana. Sprinkle with a teaspoon
of sugar.

Bake for 45 minutes until lightly firm and
golden on top.

Leave to sit for 15 minutes before serving.

Leftover porridge will last two days in an
airtight container in the fridge. Enjoy cold or
gently reheat in a warm oven.

BREAKFAST SALAD

I feel awesome when I incorporate greens and fermented vegetables like sauerkraut into my breakfast. Use this salad as a starting point and add in your favourite ingredients. Leftover roast vegetables or a half-cup of cooked grains can be tasty additions. Have the entire salad assembled before you cook the halloumi cheese as it must be piping hot when served.

4 free-range **eggs** (can be increased to 2 eggs per person if desired)
150g **baby kale leaves / rocket / mixed greens**
Extra virgin olive oil for drizzling
1 **avocado** – cut into slices
3 **radishes** – cut into wafer-thin slices
Sauerkraut – allow about ¼ cup per person
200g **halloumi cheese**
Oil for frying
1 **lemon** – cut into wedges
Cracked black pepper

TO GARNISH
Micro-greens / sprouts
Sesame seeds
Pumpkin seeds
Fresh mint leaves

Bring a saucepan of water to a boil and lower the eggs into it carefully. Cook for 6 minutes for soft-boiled eggs. Run under cold water and peel carefully.

Divide the greens between four bowls or plates. Drizzle with olive oil. Top with the avocado, radishes and sauerkraut. Cut the eggs in half and place carefully on top.

Cut halloumi into 5mm slices. Heat a couple of spoonfuls of oil in a sauté pan over a medium or high heat. Add the halloumi and cook for 1 minute on each side until golden brown.

Place on top of the salad with lemon wedges for squeezing on top. Garnish with microgreens, sesame seeds, pumpkin seeds, fresh mint and a generous grind of cracked black pepper.

42

FRESH & SALAD

Green beans w/ pistachio, rosemary & parmesan crumb	46 — GF VEG GRFR
Zucchini ribbon salad w/ goat cheese, black olives & chives	48 — GF VEG GRFR
Quinoa salad w/ edamame, avocado, capers & dill	50 — GF NF VEGN
Brussel sprout and kale slaw w/ dates, pistachios & mint	52 — DF GF GRFR VEGN
Red slaw w/ orange miso dressing & crunchy chickpeas	54 — DF GF NF VEGN
Hearty dinner salad w/ smoked salmon & baby kale	56 — DF GF NF GRFR
Nectarine, goat feta, fennel & pecan salad	58 — GF VEG GRFR
Honey & thyme roasted parsnips & baby carrots	60 — DF GF NF GRFR VEGN
The best & most simple tomato salad	60 — DF GF NF GRFR VEGN
Middle Eastern cauliflower rice pilaf	62 — DF GF GRFR VEGN
Cucumber, zucchini & carrot 'noodles' w/ creamy tahini dressing	64 — DF GF NF GRFR VEGN
Kale Caesar w/ rye croutons	66 — NF
Turmeric roasted cauliflower w/ black quinoa, raisins & pine nuts	68 — DF GF VEGN

45

GREEN BEANS
w/ pistachio, rosemary & parmesan crumb

An incredible side dish! The ridiculously tasty nut crumb works brilliantly with other vegetables, and we also love it tossed through pasta. The crumb is served at room temperature so it can be made up to three hours in advance.

Serves 4 as side

46

½ cup (65g) **raw pistachio nuts**
½ cup (50g) **raw walnuts**
Zest of 1 **lemon**
½ cup (65g) finely grated **parmesan cheese**
1 tablespoon finely chopped **rosemary leaves**
1 handful **fresh parsley leaves**
¼ teaspoon **dried chilli flakes** (optional)
Salt and **cracked black pepper**
300g **green beans** – trimmed
(can also use asparagus)
Extra virgin olive oil for drizzling

Preheat oven to 120°C (250°F). Dry-roast the nuts for 15 minutes. Set aside to cool completely.

Combine nuts, herbs, lemon zest, parmesan and chilli flakes (if using) in a food processor or blender. Season generously with salt and cracked black pepper. Blitz to the texture of coarse breadcrumbs.

Blanch or steam green beans until tender but still firm. Place on a plate or in a large bowl. Drizzle generously with olive oil and sprinkle with the nut crumb.

Serve immediately.

Leftover crumb will keep for 24 hours in an airtight container in the fridge

47

ZUCCHINI RIBBON SALAD
w/ goat cheese, black olives & chives

Raw zucchini has a fabulous texture and is a wonderful vehicle for flavour.
Combining goat cheese, salty olives and punchy chives, this dish is one you
will love alone or as part of a shared feast. We especially enjoy it with lamb or
good-quality sausages.

Dress and assemble the salad just before serving to prevent the zucchini
from becoming soggy.

3 large **zucchini**
15 **pitted black olives** – cut in half
100g **goat cheese**
Small bunch **chives**

DRESSING
45ml **extra virgin olive oil**
Juice of 1 **lemon**
1 small **garlic clove** – finely diced
1 rounded teaspoon **coconut sugar**
or **muscovado sugar** or **pure maple syrup**
Salt and **cracked black pepper**

Put the dressing ingredients into a small jar.
Season to taste with salt and cracked black
pepper. Shake vigorously until well mixed.

Trim the ends from the zucchini and use a
vegetable peeler to create ribbons. Work
around the vegetable, stopping at the seedy
core. Lay out on a tea towel for 10 minutes
to absorb some of the moisture.

Dress the zucchini with ⅔ of the dressing.
Arrange the ribbons on a platter. Crumble
the goat cheese over the top. Sprinkle with
the black olives and chives. Drizzle with the
remaining dressing as desired and garnish
with a grind of cracked black pepper.

Serve immediately.

48

4 GF NF VEGN

QUINOA SALAD
w/ edamame, avocado, capers & dill

Serve this up for dinner, make for weekday lunches or enjoy as part of a bigger meal. The simple combination of ingredients is really delicious, and will also accommodate any additions you might want to make.

1 cup (200g) **quinoa** (I've used white
but any colour will do)
2 cups (500ml) **vegetable stock**
(can also use chicken stock)
1 cup (150g) **shelled edamame beans**
(I buy these in the freezer section
of the supermarket)
1 large **avocado** (ripe but still firm is ideal)
Juice of 1 **lemon**
2 tablespoons **capers**
Large handful **fresh dill** – roughly chopped

DRESSING
60ml **extra virgin olive oil**
Juice of 1 **lemon**
1 heaped teaspoon **pure maple syrup**
or **coconut sugar**
1 large **garlic clove** – finely chopped
Salt and **cracked black pepper**

TO GARNISH
Additional fresh dill

Rinse the quinoa well and drain through a
fine sieve. Place in a medium saucepan with
the stock. Bring to a boil before reducing to
a simmer. Cook with the lid slightly ajar for
15–20 minutes until tender and the stock
has been absorbed. Let sit for 5 minutes
with the lid on.

Remove lid, fluff quinoa with a fork and leave
to cool to room temperature.

Combine the dressing ingredients in a jar
and shake vigorously until well combined.

Blanch the edamame beans by placing in
a large bowl and covering with boiling
water. Leave for 5 minutes before draining.
Remove the outer skins and discard.
Cut the avocado into cubes. Place in a bowl
and toss with the juice of 1 lemon. This will
stop the avocado going brown. Discard
extra juice.

Place the quinoa in a large bowl. Combine
with edamame beans, capers, dill and
avocado. Toss well with dressing. Season
to taste with salt and cracked black pepper.
Garnish with additional fresh dill. Serve within
an hour.

Leftovers will last up to two days in an
airtight container in the fridge.

BRUSSEL SPROUT & KALE SLAW
w/ dates, pistachios & mint

It's time to fall in love with brussel sprouts! You may have been scarred by
an earlier encounter with this little veg, but unless you've enjoyed them
thinly-sliced, raw, in a salad, you haven't seen just how great they can be.
Once the cold weather hits and lettuce isn't available anymore, you can look
to robust winter vegetables like brussel sprouts and kale to create delicious
salads. You'll need a mandoline to slice the brussel sprouts as it is essential to
have them finely and evenly chopped. I've paired these greens with gorgeously
sweet dates, mint, lemon and pistachio nuts. It's a heady combination.
Serve with a protein of your choice to create a complete meal.

52

400g medium / large **brussel sprouts**
(avoid very small ones as they're hard to slice)
5 large **kale leaves** –
sliced into very fine ribbons
½ cup (65g) **pistachio nuts** – roughly chopped
5 **Medjool dates** –
pit removed and roughly diced
Large handful **fresh mint leaves** –
roughly chopped

DRESSING
Juice of 1 juicy **lemon**
80ml **extra virgin olive oil**
1 small **garlic clove**– finely diced
1 teaspoon **Dijon mustard**
1 rounded teaspoon **pure maple syrup**
or **coconut sugar**
Salt and **cracked black pepper**

TO GARNISH
Additional pistachio nuts and mint leaves

Place the dressing ingredients in a jar.
Season generously with salt and cracked
black pepper. Put the lid on and shake
vigorously until well mixed.

Use a mandoline to slice the brussel sprouts
finely (watch your fingers!). Combine the
sprouts in a large bowl with the kale and
toss until evenly mixed. Add the dressing,
mint, dates and pistachio nuts. Mix until
everything is well coated. Leave the
salad to absorb the dressing for at least
15–20 minutes before serving. Sprinkle with
additional pistachio nuts, mint leaves and a
grind of cracked black pepper.

53

RED SLAW
w/ orange miso dressing
& crunchy chickpeas

Serve this fresh and crunchy explosion of flavour as part of a shared feast, or enjoy with a rich meat dish like my slow-and-low cooked pork shoulder (see page 126). If you don't have time to make the crunchy chickpeas – though they're addictively good – simply top with toasted seeds or chopped nuts.

54

1 x 400g can **chickpeas**–
drained and rinsed well
1 rounded teaspoon **melted coconut oil**
for roasting
¼ teaspoon **salt**
1 teaspoon **ground turmeric**
1 teaspoon **curry powder**
1 **crisp red apple** – core removed and
sliced into matchsticks with a julienne peeler
Juice of 1 **lemon**
½ **red cabbage** –
finely sliced on a mandoline
4 **radishes** – trimmed and sliced into
matchsticks (use a julienne peeler)
2 medium **carrots** – peeled and cut into
matchsticks (again, with a julienne peeler)
Large handful each of **fresh parsley** and
mint leaves – roughly chopped

DRESSING
3 tablespoons **white miso paste**
3 tablespoons **coconut cream**
or **greek yoghurt** or **mayonnaise**
1 teaspoon finely grated **ginger root**
1 teaspoon **apple cider vinegar**
Zest of 1 **orange**
Cracked black pepper

Preheat oven to 180°C (350°F).

Toss the chickpeas with the melted coconut
oil, sea salt, turmeric and curry powder.
Spread on a roasting tray lined with baking
paper. Roast for 25–30 minutes until golden
and crispy. Set aside to cool.

Whisk all the dressing ingredients together in
a small jug until smooth. Set aside until ready
to use.
Toss the cut apple in the lemon juice to
prevent browning and drain well. Combine
the apple with the cabbage, radish and
carrot in a large bowl and mix together.
Drizzle with dressing and toss until evenly
coated. Add the herbs and mix through.
Let the salad sit for 10 minutes to absorb
dressing before scattering the chickpeas on
top. Garnish with additional fresh mint leaves
if desired.

Serve immediately.

55

4 DF GF NF GRFR

HEARTY DINNER SALAD
w/ smoked salmon & baby kale

The magic lies in roast potatoes fresh from the oven, paired with a crisp, cool salad. Inspired by the classic French niçoise salad, this is a glorious one-platter meal. Place it in the middle of the table and let everyone help themselves. Tuna would be the traditional fish component but I'm a big fan of hot-smoked salmon fillets. The bright colour and rich oiliness is a pleasing combination.

56

500g **baby potatoes***
3 tablespoons **melted ghee** (see page 198)
200g **green beans** – trimmed
4 free-range **eggs***
100g **baby kale leaves** or **rocket**
or **mixed greens**
16 **Kalamata olives**
12–15 **cherry tomatoes** – halved
300g **smoked salmon fillets**
(use hot-smoked rather than cold-smoked
salmon slices) – broken into large chunks

DRESSING
Juice of 1 **lemon**
½ teaspoon **Dijon mustard**
60ml good-quality **extra virgin olive oil**
1 **garlic clove** – finely diced
Salt and **cracked black pepper**

TO GARNISH
Pumpkin seeds
Fresh dill

** Add the eggs and potatoes while hot, so prepare
just before serving.*

Preheat oven to 200°C (390°F)

Halve potatoes. Toss with melted ghee
and season generously with salt. Roast for
30–40 minutes until golden.

Combine the dressing ingredients in a
jar and shake vigorously until well mixed.
Season generously.

Trim and halve beans. Bring a saucepan
of water to boil. Add beans and cook for 1
minute before plunging into icy cold water
to cool rapidly (this helps retain the bright
green colour).

Bring another saucepan of water to boil. Add
the eggs and cook for 6 minutes (softer) or
8 minutes (hard-boiled). Run under cold
water before peeling. Cut in half.

To assemble:
Toss the leaves in two-thirds of the dressing
and scatter on a platter or large plate.
Arrange the potatoes, greens, salmon, eggs
and cherry tomatoes on top. Drizzle with
leftover dressing. Garnish with pumpkin
seeds and fresh dill. Serve immediately.

57

NECTARINE, GOAT FETA, FENNEL
& pecan salad

Pretty and fresh, this salad is a dish for any occasion. Nectarines can be
substituted with peaches or even plums.

58

100g baby spinach leaves
1 medium fennel bulb –
sliced very finely on a mandoline
100g goat feta
2 medium nectarines –
core removed and cut into wedges
Juice of 1 lemon
70g pecans – raw or lightly roasted
Handful each of fennel fronds
and fresh mint leaves – roughly chopped

DRESSING
Juice of 1 lemon
45ml extra virgin olive oil
1 rounded teaspoon coconut sugar
or pure maple syrup
1 garlic clove – finely diced
Salt and cracked black pepper

Place the dressing ingredients in a jar and
shake well to mix. Season generously with
salt and cracked black pepper. Set aside.

Pile the spinach on a large plate or platter.
Scatter the fennel and goat feta. Toss the
nectarine slices in lemon juice and arrange
on top of the salad. Drizzle salad with
dressing. Add the pecans and the herbs.
Season generously with cracked black
pepper and serve immediately.

HONEY & THYME ROASTED PARSNIPS
& baby carrots

Earthy root vegetables are enhanced with a light touch of honey and herbaceous, woody thyme. I often have to make a double batch of this recipe because I can't stop myself eating from the pan before I serve it up. The honey caramelises and creates delicious crunchy bits while the inside of the parsnips become meltingly soft. The mix of textures is irresistible.

1 bunch **baby carrots** (around 12 carrots) – trimmed and washed
3 medium / large **parsnips** – cut into sticks similar in size to the carrots
2 tablespoons **coconut oil** or **melted ghee** (see page 198), for roasting
1 tablespoon **honey / pure maple syrup**
4 **garlic cloves**
Sea salt

Preheat oven to 180°C (350°F)

Place carrots and parsnips on an oven tray. Drizzle with melted ghee and honey. Sprinkle generously with salt. Toss well. Place the garlic cloves snugly between the vegetables.

Roast for 15 minutes before turning. Roast for a further 15–20 minutes until tender and lightly golden.

60

THE BEST (AND MOST SIMPLE)
tomato salad

This is such a simple preparation, and when you have the gorgeously sweet tomatoes of high summer, you need add only the teeniest touch of seasoning to create one of my favourite salads. I love to pile it up on some good crusty bread.

500g **cherry tomatoes** – halved
2 small **garlic cloves** – finely diced
3 tablespoons **extra virgin olive oil**
1 rounded teaspoon **light muscovado sugar** or **coconut sugar**
Juice of 1 **lemon**
1 teaspoon **balsamic vinegar**
Salt and **cracked black pepper**

Combine all the ingredients in a large bowl and stir gently to combine. Place in the fridge to marinate for an hour. Stir once more before serving. Garnish with fresh basil leaves and a sprinkling of flaky sea salt.

MIDDLE EASTERN
cauliflower rice pilaf

This salad has it all. Crunch and freshness, salty olives and preserved lemons, bursts of sweetness and a herbaceousness that I adore. A fabulous way to convert those skeptical of the cauliflower's magical ability to transform into a healthy couscous substitute. Serve by itself for lunch or alongside a rich meat dish for the perfect balance. If preparing in advance, hold off adding the dressing and the avocado until just before you're ready to serve.

½ medium **cauliflower** – blitzed in a food processor until it has a rice-like texture (see page 206)
5 fresh **Medjool dates** (could use 8 dried dates) – cut finely
½ **preserved lemon** – finely diced
100g **Sicilian green olives** – pits discarded and chopped into slivers
Large handful **mint leaves** – roughly chopped
1 tablespoon **fresh thyme leaves**
⅓ cup (40g) **pistachio nuts** – roughly chopped
1 **ripe** (but still firm) **avocado** – cut into cubes
Salt and **cracked black pepper**

DRESSING
Juice of 1 **lemon**
4 tablespoons good-quality **olive oil**
1 **garlic clove** – finely diced
1 heaped teaspoon **pure maple syrup** or **coconut sugar**
Sea salt and **cracked pepper**

TO SERVE
Additional mint, fresh thyme and pistachios

Combine all dressing ingredients in a jar and shake vigorously.

Place all salad ingredients in a large bowl. Drizzle with the dressing and toss until well-coated and evenly combined. Taste and season with salt and cracked black pepper

Serve immediately. Garnish with additional mint, fresh thyme and roughly chopped pistachio nuts.

CUCUMBER, ZUCCHINI
& carrot 'noodles' w/ creamy tahini dressing

This salad is incredibly fresh and light. A julienne peeler is required to create the right texture (don't attempt this with a grater). You can pick these up fairly inexpensively at good kitchen or department stores. Serve alongside rich and fragrant dishes or use as a base for pan-fried fish or roasted chicken thighs. Toss the salad with the dressing just before serving so it doesn't go soggy.

64

1 telegraph cucumber
1 large **carrot** – trimmed and peeled
1 large **zucchini** – trimmed

DRESSING
2 tablespoons **hulled tahini**
(unhulled will also work)
1 teaspoon **white miso paste**
1 teaspoon **toasted sesame oil**
2 tablespoons **water**
1 teaspoon **coconut sugar**
or **light muscovado sugar**
Juice of 1 **lemon**
Salt and **cracked black pepper**

Trim the ends from the cucumber. Work your way around the cucumber with the julienne peeler, avoiding the seedy core.

Use the peeler to slice the carrot and zucchini as well (using the whole vegetable this time).

Lay all the vegetables out on a tea towel and blot with another tea towel or paper towels. Removing as much excess liquid as possible (especially from the cucumber) will create a crispier salad.

Place all the dressing ingredients in a small jug or bowl. Whisk until smooth. Season to taste.

Toss the salad with the dressing just before serving.

KALE CAESAR W/ RYE CROUTONS

I adore the combination of punchy Caesar dressing with robust kale leaves and the caramel richness of rye. The textures and flavours here make for a hearty and filling meal. I've skipped the traditional soft-boiled egg as I don't think it is necessary, but you can absolutely add it in along with whatever protein takes your fancy.

DRESSING
5 anchovies
1 medium **garlic clove** – finely diced
Juice of 1 **lemon**
½ cup (120–125ml) good-quality **mayonnaise**
(see page 198)
¼ cup (27g) finely grated **parmesan**

SALAD
2 x 3cm thick slices **dark rye loaf**
5 pieces free-range **streaky bacon**
8–10 large **kale leaves** – stems removed
and torn into large pieces
⅓ cup (36g) finely grated **parmesan**
for scattering
Olive oil for toasting bread and
massaging the kale
Salt and **cracked black pepper**

Preheat oven to 180°C (350°F)

Place the anchovies and garlic in a mortar,
and pestle into a rough paste. Add the
lemon juice, mayonnaise and parmesan
along with a generous grind of cracked
black pepper. Stir well and set aside until
ready to use.

Tear the bread into rough chunks. Toss with
a good drizzle of olive oil and season well
with sea salt. Bake for 10–15 minutes. You
want the croutons to be crunchy on the
outside with a soft centre.

Place a sauté pan over a medium or high
heat and cook the bacon until browned and
crispy. Tear into rough shards.

Drizzle a little olive onto the kale leaves.
Massge vigourously with your (clean) hands
for 4 minutes until softened. The leaves
will be ready when they have become dark
and glossy.

Toss the kale with the dressing (best to use
your hands here too). Arrange on a large
platter. Scatter the croutons and bacon over
the top. Sprinkle with parmesan cheese and
a little more cracked black pepper.

Serve immediately.

67

TURMERIC-ROASTED CAULIFLOWER
w/ black quinoa, raisins & pine nuts

This warm salad takes full advantage of the delightful flavour of roasted cauliflower and earthy, warming turmeric. Black quinoa has a firmness and bite that is unlike the everyday white variety. It is perfect for dishes like this.

68

Medium **cauliflower head**– cut into florets
4 tablespoons **melted coconut oil**
1 teaspoon **ground turmeric**
¼ cup (36g) **raisins** (choose a plump variety)
½ cup (100g) **black quinoa** (can also use the red or white vareties)
1 cup **vegetable stock** (can also use chicken stock)
1 **bay leaf**
⅓ cup (46g) **toasted pine nuts**
Large handful **fresh mint** – roughly chopped
Salt and **cracked black pepper**

Preheat oven to 200°C (390°F).

Place cauliflower in a large roasting dish. Toss with the coconut oil, turmeric and a generous seasoning of salt. Roast for 30 minutes, adding the raisins in the last 10 minutes of cooking, until the cauliflower tips are golden and the cauliflower is tender.

Rinse the quinoa well using a fine sieve. Place in a medium saucepan with the stock and bay leaf. Bring to a boil before reducing to a simmer. Cook for 15–20 minutes, with the lid slightly ajar until all the liquid is absorbed. Remove from heat. Place the lid on tightly and let sit for 5 minutes.

Add the quinoa to the cooked cauliflower in the roasting pan. This is a great way for it to absorb some of the flavour from the roasting process. Add the pine nuts and mint and toss well. Season generously with salt and cracked black pepper.

Serve garnished with additional mint leaves on top. Best served hot or warm.

Leftovers will last up to three days in an airtight container in the fridge. Gently reheat in a warm sauté pan.

LIGHT & LUNCH

Free-range chicken waldorf salad	72 — DF GF GRFR
Savoury muffins w/ pumpkin, thyme & feta	74 — GF VEG GRFR
Red lentil & paprika & preserved lemon soup	76 — DF GF VEGN
Mushroom, thyme & walnut pâté w/ paleo pan breads	78 — GF VEG GRFR
Crushed broad beans & peas w/ lemon & mint	80 — DF GF NF GRFR VEGN
Roasted cauliflower, rosemary & walnut soup	82 — DF GF GRFR VEGN
Chicken liver pâté w/ thyme & nutmeg	84 — GF NF GRFR
Smoked fish, chickpea, parsley & thyme salad	86 — DF GF NF
Gado Gado w/ almond butter & curry satay sauce	88 — DF GF GRFR VEGN
Zucchini noodles w/ creamy avocado sauce & smoky toasted seeds	90 — DF GF NF GRFR VEGN
Cheesy milllet balls w/ a sesame seed crumb & paprika mayo	92 — GF VEG
Ceviche w/ dill, lime & radish	94 — DF GF NF GRFR
Chickpea skillet bread w/ paprika, spring onion & parmesan	96 — GF VEG NF
Almond & buckwheat mini pizzas	98 — GF
Nori wraps w/ sunflower seed spread	100 — DF GF NF GRFR VEGN
Yoga bowl w/ roasted carrot miso & ginger dressing	102 — DF GF NF GRFR VEGN

71

FREE-RANGE CHICKEN
Waldorf salad

I have such a soft spot for this salad. It indulges my love of mayonnaise, and the crunch from the celery and apple is beautifully fresh. Served in cos lettuce leaves, it's filling but not heavy. On the days I'm craving something heartier I like to pile it onto slices of hot buttered rye toast.

72

300g free-range **chicken breast meat**
½ large **apple** – a firm and crunchy variety
Juice of 1 **lemon**
1 stalk of **celery** – thinly sliced
½ cup (50g) **walnuts** – roughly chopped
½ cup (125ml) **mayonnaise** (see page 198 or use a quality olive oil variety)
Handful **flat-leaf parsley** – roughly chopped
Oil for sautéing chicken
Salt and **cracked black pepper**
Dried red chilli flakes (optional)

TO SERVE
Baby cos leaves

Cut chicken breast in half lengthwise. Season well. Heat two tablespoons of oil in a sauté pan over a medium or high heat. Cook chicken pieces until lightly browned and no longer pink in the middle. Leave to cool before chopping into small cubes.

Cut apple into small cubes the same size as the chicken. Toss well with the lemon juice to prevent browning. Drain excess juice.

Combine chicken, celery, walnuts, parsley and mayonnaise. Mix well. Stir through apple and season well with salt and pepper.

Serve in baby cos leaves. Garnish with additional parsley leaves and a sprinkling of dried red chilli flakes if desired.

Leftover salad can be stored in an airtight container in the fridge for one day.

SAVOURY MUFFINS
w/ pumpkin, thyme & feta

I'm very much a salty or savoury person, so this is definitely my kind of baking. These muffins can fill the gap for breakfast (lightly toasted and smeared thickly with butter), as a snack while out running errands, or alongside a big bowl of soup. Throw them in the freezer and you'll be so happy you've got a stash of deliciousness on hand when you need it.

Makes 12 muffins

4 free-range **eggs** – lightly beaten
1¾ cup (195g) **almond meal**
1 **garlic clove** – finely diced
1 cup (100g) grated **cheddar cheese**
¼ cup (60ml) **melted butter**
1 heaped teaspoon **gluten-free baking powder**
1 teaspoon **ground cumin**
1 heaped teaspoon **fresh thyme leaves**
1 heaped teaspoon finely diced, **fresh rosemary leaves**
Salt and **cracked black pepper**
1½ cups **roasted pumpkin cubes***
(390g raw pumpkin cut into 2.5cm cubes will yield this once cooked)
Salt and **cracked black pepper**

TO GARNISH
Pumpkin seeds

* Roast at 180°C until tender. Do not boil the pumpkin as it will be too watery

Preheat oven to 180°C (350°F).

Combine eggs, almond meal, garlic, cheese, melted butter, baking powder, cumin and fresh herbs. This step can be done in a bowl or in a food processor. Mix until thoroughly combined. Season generously. Gently fold in roasted pumpkin.

Spoon into a well-greased or lined 12-hole muffin tin. Sprinkle with pumpkin seeds.

Bake for 25–30 minutes until golden and a skewer comes out clean when inserted.

Wait until cool before removing from the tin. Will keep for up to four days in an airtight container in the fridge.

74

RED LENTIL, PAPRIKA
& preserved lemon soup

Deeply nourishing and comforting, this soup has exquisite flavour and is very simple to make. I always soak the lentils beforehand to ensure easy digestion.

2 cups (420g) **red lentils**
1 **brown onion** – finely diced
3 **garlic cloves**– finely diced
1 teaspoon **smoked paprika** (I use hot paprika but you can also use sweet paprika)
2 teaspoons **ground cumin**
1½ teaspoons **ground turmeric**
¼ teaspoon **ground cinnamon**
2L good-quality **vegetable stock** (If you do not soak the lentils beforehand, add an additional 400mls.)
1 x 400g can **chopped tomatoes**
½ **preserved lemon** (preserved lemons usually came in quarters so use 2 pieces) – finely diced
1 tablespoon **fresh thyme leaves** (if using dried, reduce to 1 teaspoon)
Coconut oil for sautéing
Salt and **cracked black pepper**

TO SERVE
Fresh parsley leaves
Coconut yoghurt to top

Place lentils in a large bowl and cover with cold water. Leave to soak for 4–12 hours. Drain and rinse very well.

Heat a generous glug of oil in a large soup pot over medium heat. Add the garlic and onions. Sauté without browning, until tender and translucent. Add the cumin, paprika and turmeric and cook for 2 minutes. Add additional oil if the pot is too dry. Add the lentils, stock, tomatoes, preserved lemon and thyme. Bring to a boil and then reduce to a simmer. Cook for 60 minutes, stirring often. Taste and season with salt and cracked black pepper as desired.

Serve with a dollop of yogurt on top and a handful of fresh parsley leaves.

Will last up to four days in the fridge. Can be frozen for up to three months.

76

MUSHROOM, THYME & WALNUT PÂTÉ
w/ paleo pan breads

Rich earthiness and loads of goodness make this vegetarian pâté an absolute winner. Enjoy with my paleo pan breads (fresh from the skillet is delicious) or in lettuce wraps, sandwiches, in toast or with eggs.

78

1 small **garlic clove** – finely diced
250g **Portobello mushrooms** – roughly sliced
1 heaped teaspoon finely chopped **rosemary leaves**
1 teaspoon **fresh thyme leaves**
5 tablespoons **melted ghee** (see page 198) or **olive oil**
¾ cup (70g) **raw walnuts** – soaked in a large bowl of water overnight. Drained well.
Salt and **cracked black pepper**

PALEO PAN BREAD (MAKES 6)
1 cup (110g) **almond meal**
1 cup (130g) **tapioca flour**
½ cup (125ml) **almond milk**
1 free-range **egg** – lightly beaten
1 teaspoon **gluten-free baking powder**
½ teaspoon **salt**
Ghee (see page 198) / **olive oil** for frying

Heat two tablespoons of oil or ghee in a sauté pan over a medium heat. Add the garlic and cook for a minute before adding the mushrooms and herbs. Cook for 10 minutes, moving frequently, until tender and glossy. Season generously.

Combine with the remaining oil or ghee and the walnuts. Use a food processor, blender or hand blender to process until very smooth.

Best served warm or at room temperature. Drizzle with olive oil just before serving.

Will keep in an airtight container in the fridge for up to three days.

To make the paleo pan bread:
Combine all ingredients in a large bowl and mix well.

Heat a large dollop of oil in a sauté pan over medium heat. Cook the batter a quarter of a cup at a time. Spread the mixture a little each time you pour it into the pan. Cook until lightly browned on both sides.

Will last two days in the fridge in an airtight container, and can be gently reheated in the oven if desired.

CRUSHED BROAD BEANS & PEAS
w/ lemon & mint

Frozen peas and broad beans can become something rather wonderful with very little effort. I love this fresh mix of flavours on the top of hot rye toast. Create an elegant and healthy canapé by serving a dollop on a cucumber round with a shard of crispy prosciutto.

80

500g **frozen broad beans**
1 cup (150g) **frozen peas**
2 **garlic cloves** – finely diced
Juice of 2 **lemons**
3 tablespoons **extra virgin olive oil**
Handful **fresh mint leaves** – cut into fine ribbons
¾ teaspoon **sea salt**
Cracked black pepper

Place broad beans in a large bowl and cover with boiling water. Leave for 5 minutes before draining well. Remove and discard the skins.

Cover the peas in boiling water and leave for 3 minutes. Drain well and place in a food processor along with the broad beans, lemon juice, garlic, olive oil, salt and pepper. Process until the broad beans and peas are broken up but still have a little chunkiness. Add mint and pulse briefly to combine.

Can be refrigerated for up to two days. Bring to room temperature before serving.

ROASTED CAULIFLOWER, ROSEMARY
& walnut soup

I cannot urge you strongly enough to make this soup. With a delicately earthy flavour and a comforting creaminess (though it's dairy free), you'll absolutely love it. Simple enough for weeknight preparation and definitely elegant enough to serve at a dinner party. Garnish with a drizzle of extra virgin olive oil and a sprig of fresh rosemary.

82

1 medium / large **cauliflower**
1 **onion** – finely diced
3 **garlic cloves** – finely diced
1 x 400g can **cannellini beans** – drained and rinsed
1 tablespoon **rosemary leaves** – finely chopped
2L **vegetable stock** (can also use chicken stock)
¾ cup (70g) **raw walnuts**
Salt and **cracked black pepper**
Coconut oil for roasting and sautéing

Preheat oven to 200°C (390°F).

Chop cauliflower into medium-sized florets. Toss with a generous dollop of coconut oil and roast for 30–35 minutes until tender with lightly browned tips.

Heat a generous spoonful of coconut oil in a large saucepan over a medium or low heat. Add the onion and garlic. Cook for 5 minutes, without browning, until the onion is translucent. Add the cannellini beans and rosemary and cook for a further 3 minutes, stirring regularly. Add the stock, cauliflower and walnuts. Bring to a boil, before simmering for 20 minutes.

Use a blender or stick blender to puree until silky-smooth. Season to taste with salt and cracked black pepper.

CHICKEN LIVER PÂTÉ
w/ thyme & nutmeg

Liver is an incredibly nutrient-dense food and is worth of adding to your weekly menu. Pâté is my favourite way to use it. My recipe combines it with a little bacon, fresh thyme and a pinch of nutmeg. Perfect as a snack to share with friends over a glass of wine and equally wonderful for a family lunch. Great with seed crackers (see page 208), pickles and raw vegetable sticks. The ghee added to the pâté needs to be room temperature but not liquid. If liquid, place in the fridge until just solid.

84

Add a dollop of ghee to a sauté pan and place over a medium heat. Gently cook the onion and garlic for 5 minutes until tender and translucent. Add the thyme leaves in the last minute of cooking. Remove all from the pan and set aside. Add the bacon and cook over a high heat until well browned. Set aside.

Trim the livers of any sinew. Heat another spoonful of ghee in the same sauté pan and cook the livers over a high heat for 3–4 minutes on each side until lightly browned but still a little pink in the middle. Set aside to cool for 15 minutes.

½ medium onion – finely diced
1 garlic clove – finely diced
1 tablespoon fresh thyme leaves
4 rashers free-range streaky bacon
400g free-range chicken livers
(organic is even better)
½ cup (115g) room temperature ghee
(see page 198)
½ cup (125ml) good-quality chicken stock
2 pinches ground nutmeg
Salt and cracked black pepper
Additional ghee for sautéing and sealing (if desired)

Combine the livers, onion, garlic, thyme and bacon with the ghee, stock and nutmeg. Use a blender or hand blender to puree until silky-smooth. Season to taste with salt and cracked black pepper. Spoon into ramekins and place in the fridge to chill for at least two hours.

To seal with ghee or clarified butter: Spoon into desired jar or dish, removing as many air pockets as possible. Pour melted ghee on top until pâté is covered. Top with a fresh thyme sprig and place in the fridge to set.

Take the pâté from the fridge 30 minutes before serving.

The pâté will last up to a week in the fridge if under the ghee seal. Otherwise eat within three days. Can be frozen (sealed or unsealed) for up to two months.

85

SMOKED FISH, CHICKPEA, PARSLEY
& thyme salad

Fresh thyme and smoked fish is a lovely combination. Enjoy this salad on its own or pile onto thick slices of hot buttered sourdough. It's important that the salad is really well seasoned. Depending on whether the chickpeas you use are canned in brine or water, you'll need to adjust the salt levels accordingly.

86

Juice of 1 lemon
1 garlic clove – finely diced.
3 tablespoons (45ml) extra virgin olive oil
2 rounded teaspoons coconut sugar
or light muscovado sugar
150g good-quality smoked fish –
broken into chunks
1 x 400g can chickpeas –
drained and rinsed well
½ small red onion – finely diced (you'll need
¼ cup diced onion)
½ teaspoon ground cumin powder
Zest of 1 lemon
1 tablespoon fresh thyme leaves
Large handful fresh parsley –
roughly chopped
Salt and cracked black pepper

Combine the lemon juice, garlic, olive oil, sugar and a generous seasoning of salt and cracked black pepper in a jar. Place lid on and shake vigorously until well mixed. Set aside until ready to use.

Combine the smoked fish, chickpeas, red onion, cumin powder, lemon zest, parsley and thyme in a bowl. Toss with half of the dressing and season well.

Taste and add additional dressing if desired.

Serve immediately.

Leftover salad will last for one day in an airtight container in the fridge.

4-6   DF   GF   GRFR   VEGN

GADO GADO
w/ almond butter & curry satay sauce

I lived in Melbourne in my early twenties, and Gado Gado was one of my favourite things to order at the Iconic Vege Bar on Brunswick Street. This Indonesian dish of fresh vegetables with a rich satay sauce is a feast for the eyes as well as being super tasty. Plate the portions individually or serve on one large platter for a more sociable approach. The sauce is best when left for a few hours for the flavours to really meld together. Make it up to 12 hours in advance. I like some elements to be cold (tomatoes, cucumber, carrots, radish and bean sprouts) and others to be hot (broccoli, beans, eggs), but you may serve these at room temperature also if this suits you better.

88

DRESSING

½ cup (120g) almond butter (see page 202)
¼ cup (60ml) warm water
¼ cup (60ml) coconut cream
1 tablespoon tamari
1 teaspoon toasted sesame oil
Juice of 1 lime / lemon
1 teaspoon finely grated ginger
2 teaspoons coconut
or light muscovado sugar
1 teaspoon curry powder
½ teaspoon turmeric
¼ teaspoon dried chilli flakes

VEGETABLES

1 head broccoli – cut into florets
250g green beans – trimmed
4 free-range eggs (1 per person)
½ telegraph cucumber – cut into rounds
150g cherry tomatoes – halved
2 carrots – peeled, trimmed and
sliced using a julienne peeler
4 radishes – sliced thinly
2 cups bean sprouts

TO SERVE

Sesame seeds
Fresh coriander leaves
Fried shallots

Combine all the dressing ingredients in a bowl and whisk until smooth. Add additional water if you prefer a thinner sauce.

Bring a large saucepan of water to a boil. Drop the eggs carefully into the water and cook for 6 minutes (slightly soft) to 8 minutes (hard). Run under cold water before peeling and halving.

Bring another large saucepan of water to a boil. Cook the beans and broccoli for 2 minutes until just tender. Drain well.

Divide the cooked and raw vegetables among the plates. Pour the satay sauce into dipping bowls for each plate. Garnish with fresh herbs, sesame seeds and fried shallots.

Leftover satay sauce will last up to five days in the fridge in an airtight container.

89

ZUCCHINI NOODLES
w/ creamy avocado sauce
& smoky toasted seeds

It's natural to crave lighter meals in the height of summer. I serve versions of this dish often. Paprika-toasted seeds add a lovely crunch and texture to the smooth avocado sauce and crisp zucchini noodles. Perfect as is or dress it up with a piece of grilled fish or roasted chicken.

90

¼ cup (35g) raw sunflower seeds
¼ cup (35g) raw pumpkin seeds
½ teaspoon good-quality hot-smoked paprika
2 teaspoons tamari
4 medium zucchini
1 ripe avocado (ideally not over-ripe or mushy)
2 tablespoons extra virgin olive oil
1 tablespoon water
1 small garlic clove – finely diced
Handful fresh coriander – roughly chopped
Juice of 1 lime
Salt and cracked black pepper

TO SERVE
4 cherry tomatoes (halved) per person
Additional coriander leaves

Place a dry sauté pan over a medium or low heat. Add the sunflower and pumpkin seeds. Cook until lightly browned, stirring frequently (3–4 minutes). Add the paprika and cook for a further minute. Remove from the heat and drizzle with tamari. The pan will sizzle. Quickly stir the seeds to coat evenly. Set aside to cool.

Trim the zucchini and use a spiral cutter to create 'noodles'. Set aside until needed.

Use a hand blender or a small food processor to blitz the avocado, olive oil, water, garlic, coriander and lime juice until smooth and creamy. Taste and season generously with salt and pepper.

Toss the zucchini with the avocado sauce. Divide among plates. Place cherry tomatoes on top. Scatter with additional coriander and sprinkle generously with toasted seeds. Serve immediately.

Leftover dressing will last 24 hours in an airtight container in the fridge. Leftover seeds can be stored for up to two weeks in an airtight jar in the pantry.

91

CHEESY MILLET BALLS
w/ sesame seed crumb & paprika mayo

Millet is the best. It's a really versatile little grain that absorbs flavour beautifully.
I've kept this really simple flavour-wise but you could add a big handful of
chopped parsley, basil or spinach. My four-year-old daughter absolutely loves
these. The paprika mayo is an essential partner. The flavours work perfectly.

Makes 22-24 balls

MAYO
½ cup good-quality **mayonnaise**
(see page 198)
½ teaspoon good-quality **smoked paprika**

MILLET BALLS
1 cup **hulled millet**
3½ cups **vegetable stock / chicken stock**
1 medium **garlic clove** – finely diced
1 **bay leaf**
1½ cups (150g) grated **cheddar cheese**

COATING
2 free-range **eggs** – lightly beaten
¼ cup (40g) **sesame seeds**
¾ cup (85g) **almond meal**
¼ cup (35g) **tapioca flour**
Salt and **cracked black pepper**
Coconut oil / **ghee** (see page 198) for frying

Combine the mayonnaise and paprika in a small bowl. Stir well. Set aside until ready to use.

Place the millet, stock, garlic and bay leaf in a medium saucepan. Bring to a boil before reducing to a simmer. Cook with the lid slightly ajar for 20 minutes until the liquid is absorbed. The millet will be gluggy as it has absorbed a lot of extra liquid. Remove the bay leaf. Stir through the cheese and season well. Leave to cool for 15 minutes before rolling into ping-pong-sized balls. Place in the fridge to cool for at least 30 minutes.

Combine the sesame seeds, almond meal and tapioca flour in a bowl. Season with salt and pepper. Place the bowl with the beaten eggs beside it. Dip each ball into the egg and coat well with the crumb. Repeat until all the balls are coated.

Heat a very generous dollop of oil in a sauté pan over a medium or high heat. Cook in batches until well browned. Keep warm in the oven until all are cooked. Serve immediately with the mayonnaise on the side.

Leftover balls can be stored in an airtight container in the fridge for up to three days. Will freeze well for up to two weeks. Reheat (thawed) in the oven at 180°C (350°F) for 15 minutes.

93

CEVICHE W/ DILL, LIME & RADISH

Ceviche is a wonderful way to experience fresh fish. The lime juice gently 'cooks' the fish, though it retains a sweet and natural flavor. I love serving it as an appetizer. It's always a hit. Alternatively we enjoy it for supper (year round) with a tray of crispy paprika-roasted potatoes. Make sure to salt the ceviche really well just before serving. It can handle (and benefit) from more seasoning that you might think.

94

400–500g **firm white fish** – cut into 1.5cm pieces
4 tablespoons **olive oil**
½ cup (125ml) freshly squeezed **lime juice**
3 **radishes** – cut into fine matchsticks (a julienne peeler will give the best result)
1 large ripe (but firm) **avocado** – cut into cubes
Large handful **fresh dill** – roughly chopped
Salt and **cracked black pepper**

Combine fish, olive oil and lime juice in a non-metallic bowl and stir well. Place in the fridge for 30–60 minutes.

Add the radish, avocado and dill just prior to serving. Stir through gently.

Season generously with salt and a good grind of cracked black pepper.

Garnish with extra dill and micro-greens if desired. Serve immediately.

CHICKPEA SKILLET BREAD
w/ paprika, spring onion & parmesan

Chickpea flour is amazing. It has lovely flavour and enough structure to
create a tasty flatbread when paired with just water and oil. This skillet bread
is traditionally called "socca" and originates from Nice, France. It makes a
great snack to enjoy with cold drinks on a hot summer night. It's pretty good
alongside a bowl of hot soup, too. Serve immediately after cooking. It's best
piping hot from the grill.

96

1 cup (100g) **chickpea flour**
(often called besan flour)
1 cup (250ml) **water**
3 tablespoons melted **coconut oil**
or **ghee** (see page 198) or **olive oil**
¼ teaspoon **hot-smoked paprika**
¼ teaspoon **sea salt**

TO SERVE
⅓ cup (35g) finely grated parmesan
1 spring onion – finely sliced
Additional salt and cracked black pepper
1 tablespoon coconut oil / ghee for the pan

Combine the chickpea flour, water, oil,
paprika and sea salt in a bowl and whisk
until smooth. Leave the batter to sit at room
temperature for at least 30 minutes and up
to three hours.

Preheat the grill in your oven so it's hot and
ready to go.

Heat oil in a 30cm skillet (preferably one that
can go under the grill) over a medium heat.
Pour in the batter and cook for 3–4 minutes
until the top of the batter starts to dry out.
Place the skillet under the grill until browned
on top.

Sprinkle with the parmesan, spring onion,
additional salt and a good grind of cracked
black pepper. Place under the grill for a
further minute.

Cut into wedges and serve immediately.

ALMOND & BUCKWHEAT MINI PIZZAS

Pizza is always a winner. These simple no-knead bases are unusual but work
incredibly well. I enjoy making mini pizzas with this recipe but you can opt for
a couple of larger bases instead by increasing the initial cooking time slightly.
I've suggested some of my favourite combinations of toppings but go wild
and top with whatever takes your fancy.

Makes 8 (12cm) pizzas

98

1¾ cups (195g) **almond meal**
or **ground almonds**
½ cup plus 2 tablespoons (80g) **tapioca flour**
½ cup (70g) **buckwheat flour**
½ teaspoon **sea salt**
1 rounded teaspoon **gluten-free**
baking powder
½ cup (125ml) **almond / dairy milk**
¼ cup (60ml) **melted ghee** (see page 198)
or **butter**
2 free-range **eggs** – lightly beaten
1 free-range **egg white**

SOME OF MY FAVOURITE TOPPINGS
Pancetta, tomato paste and mozzarella, topped with fresh watercress or rocket and lots of cracked black pepper after cooking.

Sliced mushrooms, black olives, sliced red onion, baby spinach or kale, tomato paste, sesame seeds and a dollop of creamy hummus.

Mozzarella (no tomato) with wafer-thin slices of potato and sweet potato.

Pesto, mozzarella and slices of smoked salmon.

Garlic-infused olive oil and parmesan. Add finely chopped parsley and cracked black pepper after cooking.

Leftover bolognese sauce and mozzarella, topped with fresh basil leaves after cooking.

Preheat oven to 220°C (430°F).

Combine all ingredients in a food processor or large bowl and mix thoroughly until batter is smooth.

Line a baking sheet with baking paper. Pour ¼ cup of batter onto the sheet and use a wide knife or thin spatula to spread it out until 12cm wide, round, and slightly less than 1cm thick. Repeat this process as many times as you can fit onto the sheet (probably 3–4 pizza bases). Bake for 10 minutes. Cool the finished bases on a wire rack. Repeat the process until all the batter is used.

Garnish bases with toppings of your choice and bake for 10–12 minutes.

Bases can be stored in an airtight container for up to two days until ready to use or can be frozen for up to a month.

99

NORI WRAPS
w/ sunflower seed spread

During the warmer months, I could eat this at every meal. My sunflower seed spread is a rich and savoury plant-based delight. The humble sunflower seed is filled with goodness, and this is such a delicious way to enjoy it. Nori sheets (dried seaweed) make the perfect alternative to bread wraps and deliver a healthy dose of iodine and other minerals. I've listed some ideas for fillings but use whatever your heart desires.

SPREAD
1 cup (140g) raw sunflower seeds –
soaked for 12 hours in a large bowl of water.
Drained and rinsed well.
¼ cup (60ml) good-quality olive oil
1 teaspoon pure maple syrup or coconut sugar
1 tablespoon tamari
1 teaspoon savoury yeast flakes
(also called nutritional yeast)
1 tablespoon fresh thyme leaves
1–6 tablespoons water (as needed)
Salt and cracked black pepper
Juice of 1 lemon

TO ASSEMBLE ROLLS
Nori sheets – allow 1–2 per person
Avocado
Greens (baby spinach, baby kale,
watercress, rocket etc.)
Sauerkraut
Shredded carrot
Fresh herbs as desired (roughly chopped
parsley, mint and basil are all good)

Combine all sunflower seed spread ingredients in a powerful blender or food processor (a hand blender works well too). Process until as smooth as possible (adding water only as needed). Season to taste.

To assemble:
Lay out the nori sheets. Spread the first third with the sunflower spread. Place the other ingredients on top, keeping to that section. Tightly roll the nori sheets, using a drop of water to secure the roll. Cut in half and serve.

100

YOGA BOWL
w/ roasted carrot, miso & ginger dressing

This grounding bowl of goodness can be customised to include whatever vegetables or protein you have on hand. The dressing is incredibly addictive. You'll want to pour it on everything.

102

DRESSING

1 large **carrot** (or 2 medium)
2 tablespoons **white miso paste**
¼ cup (60ml) **light olive oil**
Juice of 1 **lemon**
1 teaspoon **sesame oil**
1 teaspoon finely grated **ginger**
½ cup (125ml) **water** (or more, as needed)
1 teaspoon **melted coconut oil** for roasting

SALAD

½ cup (100g) **black** or **white quinoa**
or **hulled millet**
1 cup (250ml) **vegetable stock**
(can also use chicken stock)
½ **clove garlic** – finely diced
½ small head of **broccoli**
2 handfuls **watercress / other salad leaves**
½ ripe (but firm) **avocado** – sliced
1 **radish** – sliced thinly
2 **button mushrooms** – sliced thinly
¾ cup **sprouts**
½ cup **sauerkraut**

TO GARNISH

Black and white sesame seeds

Preheat oven to 180°C (350°F).

Peel carrot and cut into large chunks. Toss with the coconut oil. Roast for 35 minutes or until tender. Place in a blender or use a hand blender to puree along with the other dressing ingredients until very smooth. Add extra water if needed. The dressing will thicken quite a lot when cooled.

Place the quinoa, stock and garlic in a small saucepan. Bring to a boil before reducing to a simmer. Cook with the lid ajar for 15–20 minutes until it's tender and the liquid has been absorbed. Place the lid on firmly and leave to sit for 5 minutes before fluffing with a fork.

Cut the broccoli into florets and steam until just tender.

Divide the cooked quinoa between two bowls or plates. Split the salad greens, broccoli, avocado, radish slices, mushrooms, sprouts and sauerkraut between the dishes.

Drizzle with a little of the dressing and serve with more on the side. Thin the dressing with a little more water if it has thickened too much. Garnish with black and white sesame seeds.

Leftover dressing will last up to four days in a jar in the fridge.

103

MAIN & DINNER

Succulent slow-braised lamb neck chops	106 — DF GF NF GRFR
Beef, red wine & prune pot pies w/ paleo pastry	108 — GF GRFR
Ultimate Bolognese	110 — DF GF NF GRFR
Pork & fennel meatballs w/ simple tomato sauce	112 — DF GF GRFR
Creamy chicken saag	114 — DF GF NF GRFR
Vietnamese fish w/ turmeric & dill	116 — DF GF NF GRFR
Rosemary & thyme meatloaf	118 — DF GF GRFR
Punchy pork larb	120 — DF GF NF
Paleo lasagne w/ creamy cauliflower sauce & sweet potato layers	122 — DF GF GRFR
Lamb & white bean burgers	124 — DF GF NF
Slow & low-cooked pork shoulder w/ sweet & salty spice rub	126 — DF GF NF GRFR
Pistachio, lemon & parsley-crusted salmon	128 — DF GF GRFR
Almond & black sesame-crusted fish tacos w/ sambal oelek mayo	130 — DF GF
Lightly spiced chicken drumsticks w/ lemon & coriander	132 — DF GF NF GRFR
Creamy buckwheat risotto w/ roasted broccoli & pine nuts	134 — GF VEG
Vegan nachos w/ sweet potato chips	136 — DF GF NF VEGN
Sweet potato gnocchi w/ broccoli, macadamia & basil pesto	138 — DF GF VEG
Mac 'n' cheese w/ creamy cauliflower sauce	140 — GF VEG NF
Tamarind coconut & lentils	142 — DF GF NF VEGN
Creamy parsnip risotto w/ mushrooms	144 — GF VEG NF GRFR
Smoky & spicy spanish beans w/ paprika & saffron	146 — DF GF NF VEGN
Weeknight noodles	148 — DF GF VEG NF
Zucchini noodle ramen w/ miso-roasted eggplant & perfect soft-boiled eggs	150 — DF GF NF GRFR VEGN
Creamy leek, chard & tarragon tart w/ buckwheat & brown rice crust	152 — GF VEG NF

105

SUCCULENT SLOW-BRAISED
lamb neck chops

This is the kind of meal I love to make for my dad. It makes his Irish heart melt. Lamb neck is an under-rated and inexpensive cut of meat that becomes incredibly rich and unctuous with low and slow cooking. The braising process unlocks the goodness of the bones and marrow as well, creating a nourishing broth. Enjoy with a root vegetable mash and green vegetables.

Preheat oven to 150°C (300°F).

Heat two tablespoons of ghee or oil in a sauté pan over a medium heat. Add the onions and garlic and cook gently for 5 minutes without browning until translucent. Add the anchovies and move them gently around the pan for a minute or two until they've mostly melted into the onion. Stir through the preserved lemon. Remove from heat and reserve until ready.

Add the remaining oil to the pan and increase the heat to high. Season the chops well and brown in batches of three or four at a time. Avoid overcrowding the pan. Sear the fat that surrounds each chop as this adds wonderful flavour.

Place the browned chops in a large casserole dish and spoon over the onions and garlic. If the casserole dish is suitable for the stovetop, pour in the stock and passata and bring to a boil. Alternatively, bring the stock and passata to a boil in a large saucepan. Pour over the meat in the casserole dish. Scatter the thyme leaves.

Cook with the lid on for 3.5 hours until the meat is meltingly tender and coming away from the bone. Gently pour the liquid from the casserole dish into a medium saucepan. Make a paste with the tapioca flour and a little water. Whisk into the cooking liquid and bring to a boil. Simmer for 20 minutes until glossy and thickened. Put back into the casserole dish.

Handle the chops very gently when serving as they fall apart very easily. Leftovers can be stored in an airtight container in the fridge for up to three days. Reheat with a little cooking liquid in a covered sauté pan.

Can be frozen for up to two months.

1 **brown onion** – finely chopped
4 **garlic cloves** – finely chopped
8 **anchovies**
¼ **preserved lemon** – finely diced
1.2kg **lamb neck chops** (10–12 pieces)
1L good-quality **beef stock**
¾ cup (185ml) **tomato passata**
1 tablespoon **fresh thyme leaves**
1 tablespoon **tapioca flour**
3 tablespoons **ghee** (see page 198)
or **coconut oil** for sautéing and browning
Salt and **cracked black pepper**

107

BEEF, RED WINE & PRUNE
pot pies w/ paleo pastry

Pies are a truly Kiwi comfort food. They are practically our national dish.
My take on the classic will satisfy all your pie yearnings while still being
wholesome. Use a nice wine for the beef – one you won't mind drinking while
you cook. It does make a difference.

The meat component can be made a couple of days in advance and the
pastry dough up to 24 hours beforehand. Note that a large pie will take
slightly longer than a small pie to cook.

Preheat oven to 150°C (300°F)

Cut beef into 2.5cm cubes (roughly). Heat a generous glug of oil in a heavy-bottomed casserole dish over a medium or high heat. Brown the beef in batches and set aside.

Add a little more oil to the dish and reduce heat. Sauté the onion, garlic, carrot and celery, without browning, until the onion is tender and translucent. Add the fennel seeds in the last 2 minutes. Add the meat to the casserole dish along with the stock, wine, bay leaf, thyme and prunes. Turn the heat up and bring to a boil.

Place in the oven with lid on. Cook for 2.5 hours until meltingly tender. Mix the tapioca with a little cold water to create a paste. Stir through the casserole and cook for a further 30–40 minutes uncovered until thickened.

The casserole can be stored in the fridge for up to four days until you're ready to make the pies. Will store in freezer for three months. Thaw completely in the fridge before using.

1.2kg **stewing beef** – I like to use gravy beef
1 large **brown onion** – finely diced
4 **garlic cloves** – finely diced
2 medium **carrots** – finely diced
1 stalk **celery** – finely diced
1 teaspoon **fennel seeds**
1 tablespoon **fresh thyme leaves**
3 cups (750ml) good-quality **beef stock**
¾ cup (185ml) **red wine**
1 **bay leaf**
9 **prunes** – halved
2 tablespoons **tapioca flour**
Oil for sautéing

PALEO PASTRY
¾ cup (85g) **almond meal**
½ cup (65g) **tapioca flour**
2 tablespoons **coconut flour**
½ teaspoon **sea salt**
2 tablespoons **cold ghee** (see page 198) – from the fridge
2 medium free-range **eggs**
1–2 tablespoons of **cold water** (as necessary)

To make the pastry:
Preheat oven to 180°C (350°F).

Place all the ingredients except water and egg into a food processor. Blitz until it is the texture of coarse breadcrumbs. Add the eggs and process for another minute. Add the water only if necessary, one tablespoon at a time. The dough is ready when it comes together in a ball (only just). Wrap the dough ball in cling film and place in the fridge for at least 30 minutes, and up to 24 hours.

Take the pastry dough from the fridge and flatten slightly. Place between two pieces of baking paper and roll out until 1 cm thick. Trace the outer rim of the dish or dishes you are using for the pies to cut out the pastry tops.

Spoon the cold pie filling into the dishes. Lay the pastry on top and use a fork to flatten the outer edges. Prick the centre of the pastry a few times.

Bake for 30–40 minutes until golden brown and crisp.

109

ULTIMATE BOLOGNESE

Our family loves Bolognese and I think this is my best version. The bacon adds a richness that means a little goes a long way. You might be a bit intimidated to see free-range liver appear in the ingredients but truly it adds wonderful nourishment and depth to the dish. The liver is diced into very small pieces and cooked over a high heat until almost caramelized. It is virtually unrecognisable in the end result but the whole thing has a big, bold flavour.

Rather than choosing between zucchini noodles and gluten-free pasta, I use both!

110

150g **chicken livers** – I prefer to use organic
or at least free-range
1 **brown onion** – finely diced
2 **garlic cloves** – finely chopped
1 teaspoon **fennel seeds**
800g **beef mince**
125g streaky free-range **bacon** – diced
3 x 400g cans **cherry tomatoes**
1 tablespoon **fresh rosemary leaves** –
finely chopped
1 tablespoon **fresh thyme leaves**
1 cup (250ml) **beef stock**
½ cup (125ml) **red wine**
Salt and **cracked black pepper**
Ghee (see page 198) / **olive oil** for sautéing

Wash the livers and pat dry with paper towel. Trim off any visible sinew and dice into very small pieces. It's important to take the time to dice well so you don't end up with discernable liver chunks. Heat a large spoonful of oil in a sauté pan over a medium or high heat. Add the chopped liver and cook for about 5 minutes until it is deeply browned. Don't be afraid to let it get a really dark colour. Remove from the pan, adding a splash of water to help scrape up all the caramalised pieces that have stuck to the pan.

Reduce the heat to medium. Add another large spoonful of oil along with the onions and garlic. Cook gently until tender and translucent. Add the fennel seeds and cook for a further minute. Turn the heat up slightly and add the bacon. Cook for 3 minutes until the fat has started to melt from the bacon.

111

Turn the heat up to high and add the mince. Cook for 10–15 minutes until it is well browned and some of the fat has cooked off. Do not try to shorten this step. Your end result could end up too oily.

Add the liver, tomatoes, stock, wine and herbs. Bring to a boil, before reducing the heat to medium and simmering for one hour. Add a little water or more stock if the pan becomes dry.

Taste and season generously, as required, with salt and cracked black pepper.

Though not traditional, a cup or two of diced Portobello mushrooms or two large handfuls of chopped greens work brilliantly in here, too.

PORK AND FENNEL MEATBALLS
w/ simple tomato sauce

Pork and fennel is a classic combination for good reason. These tasty little meatballs are great for a midweek family meal and perfect for a casual dinner with friends. I like to serve them atop some sautéed garden greens. You could also pair with gluten-free pasta or broccoli 'rice'.

112

MEATBALL
2 teaspoons **fennel seeds**
600g free-range **pork mince**
1 free-range **egg** – lightly beaten
¾ cup (85g) **almond meal**
1 teaspoon **sea salt**
¼ teaspoon **dried red chilli flakes**
Large handful **fresh parsley leaves** –
roughly chopped

SAUCE
400g **tomato passata sauce**
½ **onion** – finely diced
1 small **garlic clove** – finely diced
1 rounded teaspoon **muscovado**
or **coconut sugar**
Salt and **cracked black pepper**
Ghee (see page 198) / **other oil** for sautéing

Combine all the meatball ingredients in a large bowl and use your hands to mix well. Roll heaped tablespoons of mixture into balls and place in the fridge until ready to use.

Heat a generous dollop of oil in a sauté pan over a medium heat. Add the onion and garlic. Cook without browning for 5 minutes until translucent. Add the passata and sugar. Simmer for 15 minutes. Season generously.

Heat a generous dollop of oil in another sauté pan over a medium or high heat. Cook the meatballs in two batches to avoid overcrowding the pan. Ensure they are nicely browned and no longer pink in the middle.

You can either add the meatballs to the sauce and let them heat in the sauce for a few minutes, or heat the components separately and serve the meatballs on top of the sauce.

Leftover meatballs and sauce will last three days in an airtight container in the fridge.

CREAMY CHICKEN SAAG

I've always loved this Indian curry (our go-to comfort food). It is so easy to re-create at home. I use frozen spinach because I always have some on hand and it makes the dish very quick to pull together.

1 **onion** – finely diced
1 tablespoon finely grated **ginger**
4 large **garlic cloves** – finely diced
1 tablespoon **ground cumin**
1 teaspoon **garam masala**
½ teaspoon **ground turmeric**
¼ teaspoon **cayenne pepper**
500g **frozen spinach leaves**
1 x 400g can **chopped tomatoes**
1 x 400g can **coconut cream**
1½ cups (375ml) **vegetable stock**
½ teaspoon **salt**
Juice of 1 **lime**
800g free-range **chicken thighs** – cut into chunks
Salt and **cracked black pepper**
Coconut oil for sautéing

TO SERVE
Millet, brown rice or quinoa

Heat a generous dollop of oil in a sauté pan over medium heat. Add the onion, ginger and garlic. Cook until the onion is translucent and tender. Add the spices and cayenne pepper. Stir for a further minute, adding more oil if the pan is dry.

Add the spinach (fine to add it frozen), tomatoes, salt, coconut cream and stock. Bring to a boil and stir until the spinach has thawed and is thoroughly combined. Simmer for 10 minutes. Stir through the lime juice.

Place in a food processor or blender and blitz until the spinach is finely chopped and the sauce is green. A blender will give a very fine result and a food processor a more roughly chopped sauce.

Heat a very generous dollop of oil in a sauté pan over a high heat. Add the chicken and cook for 2 minutes on both sides until browned. Add the spinach sauce and simmer for 10 minutes.

Serve with steamed millet, brown rice or quinoa. Leftover curry will last two days in an airtight container in the fridge.

VIETNAMESE FISH
w/ turmeric & dill

This is one of my absolute favourite dishes. A wonderfully surprising combination of flavours. The large amount of fish sauce combined with curry powder, turmeric and handfuls of dill might look unusual at first but I really urge you to try it – it's exquisite and simple to put together. Even my four-year-old daughter loves it. It would traditionally be served with rice noodles but we most often pair it with cauliflower rice.

116

500g firm **white fish fillets**
4 **spring onions**
2 **garlic cloves**
1 rounded teaspoon **ground turmeric**
1 rounded teaspoon **curry powder**
2 tablespoons **yoghurt**
3 tablespoons **fish sauce**
2 tablespoons **coconut sugar**
or **demerara sugar**
2 tablespoons **light olive oil**
1 bunch **dill**
½ cup (125ml) **fish stock**
(can also use chicken stock in a pinch)
250g **green beans** – trimmed
Oil for sautéing

TO SERVE
Lime wedges
Bean sprouts

Cut the fish into 3cm pieces. Combine the white part of the spring onions and the garlic cloves in a mortar, and pestle into a rough paste. Combine in a large bowl with the fish sauce, turmeric, curry powder, yoghurt, sugar and oil. Gently toss the cut fish through this marinade. Roughly chop a third of the dill and stir through. Leave to marinate for at least an hour and up to 8 hours.

Just before you cook the fish, blanch the beans for 1 minute. Drain well and set aside.

Heat a spoonful of oil in a pan over a high heat. Use tongs or a slotted spoon to remove the fish from the marinade and add to the pan. You don't want to have all the marinade enter the pan as the end result will be too salty. Cook fish for 1 minute before flipping. Add the fish stock, reduce to a medium heat and cook for 3–5 minutes.

Lay the beans out on a platter or large plate. Spoon the fish and liquid over the top. Scatter a handful of bean sprouts on top. Finely slice the leftover green part of the spring onions and roughly chop the remaining dill. Sprinkle on top of fish and serve immediately with lime wedges.

117

ROSEMARY & THYME MEATLOAF

Meatloaf might seem a tad old-fashioned but I've got a really soft spot for it – especially when it's packed with garlic and fresh herbs. It's wonderful for family dinners and the plentiful leftovers can become lunches and quick meals. Reheat slices in a hot pan or enjoy cold in a ploughman's platter. Serve with a pile of steamed green vegetables or a big salad.

118

1 **brown onion** – finely diced
4 **garlic cloves** – finely diced
2 medium **carrots** – peeled and grated
1 tablespoon finely diced **fresh rosemary leaves**
1 tablespoon **fresh thyme leaves**
800g **beef mince**
500g free-range **pork mince**
⅓ cup (45g) **tapioca flour**
2 tablespoons **Worcestershire sauce**
2 free-range **eggs** – lightly beaten
1 teaspoon **sea salt**
Salt and **cracked black pepper**
8 rashers free-range **streaky bacon**
Ghee (see page 198) **/ other oil** for sautéing

Heat a generous dollop of oil in a sauté pan over a medium heat. Add the onion, garlic and carrot. Cook for 5–7 minutes, without browning, until the onion is translucent and tender. Add the rosemary and thyme in the last 2 minutes of cooking. Set aside to cool.

Preheat oven to 180°C (350°F).

Combine cooled onion mixture in a large bowl with the beef mince, pork mince, tapioca flour, Worcestershire sauce, eggs, salt and a generous grind of cracked black pepper.

Line a 24cm loaf tin with baking paper. I pre-grease the tin with butter before lining, to ensure the paper fits very tightly.

Lay five slices of bacon side-by-side across the bottom of the tin. Press the meat mixture in until it is snug in the tin, and use your hands to smooth out the top. Spread three slices of bacon lengthways across the top and tuck in at the ends.

Bake for 70 minutes. Let the loaf sit for 15–20 minutes before slicing.

Leftovers will last three days in an airtight container in the fridge.

119

PUNCHY PORK LARB

I'm a huge fan of the balanced nature of Thai dishes. That hit of chilli with
a little sweetness and the brightness of lime is something I often crave. Larb
is an incredibly fast midweek meal. I love heat, but you can halve the
chilli if you prefer a milder approach. This dish will work with free-range
minced chicken too.

1½ tablespoons **jasmine rice**
1½ tablespoons **fish sauce**
2 teaspoons **coconut sugar**
or **light muscovado sugar**
Juice of 2 **limes**
1 stem **lemongrass** –
white part only, finely sliced
2 large **red chillies** –
de-seeded and finely sliced
500g free-range **pork mince**
1 **spring onion** – sliced
Large handful **fresh coriander** –
roughly chopped
Handful **fresh mint** –
roughly chopped
1 tablespoon **oil** for sautéing

TO SERVE
Cos leaves
Additional coriander
Sticky rice

Place a dry sauté pan over a medium heat.
Add the rice and cook, moving frequently,
until lightly golden. Place in a mortar, and
pestle into a coarse powder. Set aside.

Combine the fish sauce, sugar and lime
juice in a small jug and stir well. Set aside.

Heat 1 tablespoon of oil in a sauté pan over
a medium or high heat. Add the lemongrass,
chilli and pork mince. Cook for 7–10 minutes
until the pork is no longer pink in the middle.
Add the ground rice and cook for a minute.
Add the fish sauce dressing and remove
from the heat. Toss through the spring
onion, coriander and mint.

Scoop the larb into cos leaves and serve
immediately with coriander and sticky rice on
the side (if desired).

PALEO LASAGNE
w/ creamy cauliflower sauce
& sweet potato layers

Whether or not you are interested in paleo eating, my version of the
Italian comfort food classic is super delicious. Cauliflower puree stands in
seamlessly for béchamel sauce. Wafer-thin slices of sweet potato replace
pasta, so it's texture isn't quite as firm as the traditional version. It's essential
to use a mandolin to slice the sweet potato so that it's thin enough to cook
properly. This recipe takes a little while to put together but is well worth
the effort.

122

Heat a generous spoonful of oil in a sauté pan over medium heat. Add the onion, garlic and carrot. Cook gently until the onion is translucent. Add the beef; raise the heat to high and cook, moving frequently, until well browned. Don't rush this stage. It will give a rich end result.

Add the passata or tinned tomatoes, stock, cumin and thyme. Bring to a boil before reducing to a simmer for 60 minutes. You want this to be a much dryer result than a traditional Bolognese sauce as there won't be pasta in the lasagna to soak up excess liquid. Season generously.

BEEF RAGU
1 brown onion – finely diced
2 large garlic cloves – finely diced
1 large carrot – peeled and finely diced
800g beef mince
2 cups tomato passata
or 2 x 400g tins chopped tomatoes
¾ cup (185ml) beef stock
1 teaspoon ground cumin
1 tablespoon fresh thyme leaves
or 1 teaspoon dried thyme

CAULIFLOWER SAUCE
½ brown onion – finely diced
1 large garlic clove – finely diced
1 medium head cauliflower – cut into florets
1 cup (250ml) vegetable / chicken stock
3 tablespoons olive oil

Heat a generous dollop of oil in another sauté pan over a medium heat. Add the onion and garlic. Cook gently until the onion is tender and translucent. Add the cauliflower and stock. Cover, turn heat to low and cook for 15–20 minutes until very soft. Turn heat down if it starts to bubble over. Place the cauliflower and stock into a blender (or use a stick blender). Add the olive oil and season generously with salt and cracked black pepper. Puree until silky smooth.

123

Preheat oven to 180°C (350°F).

TO ASSEMBLE
2–3 medium sweet potatoes (orange kumara) – sliced very thinly on a mandolin
Salt and cracked black pepper
Ghee (see page 198) / coconut oil for sautéing and brushing top layer of sweet potato.
3 tablespoons almond meal
1 tablespoon sesame seeds
2 tablespoons sunflower seeds
2 tablespoons pumpkin seeds

TO SERVE
Steamed green vegetables / green salad

Grease an ovenproof lasagne dish. Place a layer of sweet potato slices (tiled tightly) on the bottom. Top with half the ragu. Gently spread half the cauliflower sauce on top. Cover with another layer of tiled sweet potato slices, then the rest of the ragu followed by cauliflower sauce. Top with the final layer of sweet potato. Brush the slices with oil. Combine the almond meal, sesame seeds, sunflowers seeds and pumpkin seeds. Sprinkle this over the lasagne and season with sea salt and cracked black pepper.

Bake for 45–50 minutes until the sweet potato is golden and crispy. Leave to stand for 15 minutes before serving.

Serve with steamed green vegetables or a green salad.

Leftovers will last up to four days in an airtight container in the fridge.

LAMB & WHITE BEAN BURGERS

Adding white beans to these burger patties gives a lighter feel and softer texture. They never dry out and for those who are not hugely carnivorous, it is a slightly less intense burger. I serve them in fresh lettuce leaves and pile on my favourite toppings.

Makes 15 burgers

1 x 400g can **cannellini beans** – drained and rinsed well
1 large **garlic clove** – finely diced
600g **lamb mince**
1 free-range **egg**
½ teaspoon **salt**
½ teaspoon **dried oregano**
Oil / **ghee** (see page 198) for cooking patties

TO SERVE
Iceberg / cos lettuce leaves (allow a few per person)
Radish slices
Sliced avocado
Mayonnaise
Grated carrot
Micro-greens / watercress
Finely chopped chives

Place the beans and garlic in a food processor and blitz you achieve a smooth paste. Add the lamb mince, egg, salt and oregano. Process briefly to bring the mixture together. Do not overmix.

Roll heaped spoonfuls into patties. The mixture will be very sticky. Damp hands will make it easier. Stack the patties on a plate and place in the fridge to firm up for 30–60 minutes.

Heat a generous spoonful of oil over a medium heat in a sauté pan. Cook the patties for 5 minutes on each side until they are browned and the juices run clear when the patty is pressed.

Store the cooked patties covered in a warm oven until all the patties are ready.

Lay out the salad ingredients and condiments on a large platter. Place the patties in the centre of the table and allow guests to build their own burgers.

Leftover burger patties will last up to three days in an airtight container in the fridge.

124

SLOW AND LOW-COOKED
pork shoulder w/ sweet & salty spice rub

Our family gets very excited when this goes into the oven. We find it hard to wait the six hours until it is ready. The outside has a crunchy crust and the inside is meltingly tender. Serve with homemade fries and one of my slaw recipes, wrap up in an iceberg lettuce leaf with avocado and pickles or eat straight from the pan.

126

1 teaspoon **coriander seeds**
1 teaspoon **fennel seeds**
1 teaspoon **cumin seeds**
1 tablespoon **sugar** (any variety will work)
1 tablespoon **sea salt**
1.2kg free-range **pork shoulder** (bone in)

Preheat oven to 140°C (285°F).

Place a dry skillet over a medium or low heat. Add the coriander seeds, fennel seeds and cumin seeds. Toast for 1–2 minutes, moving frequently, until fragrant.

Grind seeds in a mortar and pestle until the texture of a coarse flour. Add the sugar and salt and grind until the texture is relatively even.

Place the pork shoulder in a roasting dish and spread the rub all over it. Place in the oven for six hours. You can spoon the cooking juices over the meat every hour or so if you wish or just leave it for the entire cooking time. Let the shoulder sit for 20 minutes when you take it out of the oven, before shredding into large chunks.

PISTACHIO, LEMON &
parsley-crusted salmon

This is a beautiful and simple way to serve nutritious salmon. It's also a great way to feed a crowd. Just double (or triple) the crumb recipe and salmon. You can fit lots of portions on the one oven tray. I've served this to groups of 12–30 guests (you just need enough oven space!). It looks lovely and is a real cinch if you prep the salmon pieces in advance. Pair with some great salads and your guests will be very impressed.

½ cup (70g) **raw pistachio nuts**
Zest of 1 **lemon**
⅓ cup (20g) (tightly packed) **fresh parsley**
¼ teaspoon **sea salt**
1 free-range **egg white**
4 x 150g **salmon fillets**– ask your fishmonger to de-bone for you

Preheat oven to 200°C (390°F).

Place the pistachios, lemon zest, parsley and salt in a food processor or blender and blitz untilthe texture is that of coarse breadcrumbs.

Brush each piece of salmon with egg white. Spoon crumb over each piece and lightly press with your hand.

Roast for 12 minutes. The salmon should be only just done (as it will continue to cook with the residual heat) and flake easily.

Serve immediately.

ALMOND & BLACK SESAME
crusted fish tacos w/ sambal oelek mayo

Fish tacos are a little bit heavenly, aren't they? The combination of fresh fish, warm corn tortillas and crunchy vegetables is perfect. My version strays from traditional Mexican flavours, instead incorporating one of my most-loved condiments: sambal oelek, an addictive Southeast Asian sauce made with chillies, onion and garlic. I put it on everything! Here I've used it to make a punchy mayonnaise. The fish is coated in a mix of ground almonds, black sesame seeds and cumin.

Be generous with the fresh mint and chilli when serving.
They really make the dish sing.

130

⅓ cup (80ml) good-quality **mayonnaise**
(see page 198)
1 heaped teaspoon **sambal oelek**
(purchase from Asian stores or the
Asian section of good grocers)
¾ cup (85g) **almond meal / ground almonds**
4 teaspoons **black sesame seeds**
½ teaspoon **ground cumin**
salt and **cracked black pepper**
1 free-range **egg** – lightly beaten
400g firm **white fish** – cut into
finger-sized pieces
Ghee (see page 198) / **coconut oil**
for shallow frying
2–3 **soft corn tortillas** per person.
3 **radishes** – very finely sliced
80g **microgreens / watercress**

TO GARNISH
Additional sesame seeds
Fresh mint leaves
Dried red chilli flakes
Cracked black pepper
Fresh lime wedges.

Mix the mayonnaise and sambal oelek.
Set aside until ready to use.

Combine the almond meal, black sesame
seeds, cumin and salt and pepper in a bowl.
Mix well.

Place the egg in a bowl beside this. Dip the
fish pieces in the egg and then in the crumb
and press to coat well. Repeat until all the
fish is coated.

Heat oil (2cm deep) over a medium or high
heat, in a sauté pan. Once it is piping hot,
add the fish (you will need to do this in 2–3
batches), and cook for a minute or so on
each side until golden. Keep the cooked
fish warm in the oven until you have finished
cooking it all.

Heat the tortillas according to the packet
instructions – I like to use a dry skillet and
lightly wet each tortilla. However this can
take a little while, and you may prefer to
warm a whole batch in the oven.

You can assemble the tacos in advance or
place all the ingredients on a platter on the
table and have each person build their own.

To assemble: Place 1–2 pieces of fish on
each warm tortilla. Top with a liberal blob
of mayonnaise. Top with radish slices and
greens. Sprinkle generously with mint leaves,
sesame seeds, chilli flakes and cracked
black pepper. Squeeze lime juice over the
top just before eating.

131

LIGHTLY SPICED CHICKEN DRUMSTICKS
w/ lemon & coriander

Chicken drumsticks are a firm family favourite. So simple and full of flavour. We like to pair this with buttery steamed broccoli and homemade sauerkraut.

132

1kg free-range **chicken drumsticks**
1 teaspoon **ground turmeric**
1 teaspoon good-quality **hot-smoked paprika**
1 **lemon** – cut into thin slices
Handful **fresh coriander** – roughly chopped
Salt and **cracked black pepper**

Preheat oven to 180°C (350°F).

Place the drumsticks in a large bowl and sprinkle with turmeric and paprika. Season generously with salt and pepper. Toss until evenly coated.

Place the chicken in an ovenproof dish. Lay the lemon slices over the top. Bake for 45 minutes or until the juices run clear. Remove from the oven and sprinkle fresh coriander over the top.

CREAMY BUCKWHEAT RISOTTO
w/ roasted broccoli & pine nuts

Buckwheat can be transformed into the most heavenly risotto with just a little bit of love. Soaking beforehand helps to soften its strong flavour and ensure it cooks down to a beautifully tender texture. I love the salty crispness of roasted broccoli, but feel free to play around with other pairings. Roasted cauliflower and smoked salmon are both tasty additions.

134

1 cup (180g) **raw buckwheat groats**
2 medium **broccoli heads** – cut into florets
3 **garlic cloves** – finely diced
1 **leek** – trimmed and finely sliced
½ teaspoon **dried tarragon**
or 1 teaspoon **fresh thyme leaves**
½ cup (125ml) **white wine**
Zest of 1 **lemon**
1 **bay leaf**
3½ cups (875ml) **vegetable stock**
(can also use chicken stock)
½ cup (60g) finely grated **parmesan cheese**
Oil – 3 tablespoons each
for sautéing and roasting
Salt and **cracked black pepper**

TO SERVE
Extra parmesan
Toasted pine nuts

Place buckwheat in a large bowl and cover with cold water. Leave to soak overnight or for at least eight hours. Drain and rinse well under running water until no longer gluggy. Set aside.

Preheat oven to 200°C (390°F). Place the broccoli in an ovenproof dish. Toss well with oil and roast until just tender with browned tips. Season generously with salt.

Heat three tablespoons of oil in a sauté pan over a medium heat. Add the garlic and leeks. Cook gently, without browning, until translucent.

Add the tarragon, white wine, buckwheat, lemon zest, bay leaf and roughly half the stock. Reduce the heat slightly and cook until the liquid is almost entirely all absorbed – stirring often. Remove the bay leaf after 15 minutes. Continue to add the stock in half cup (125ml) increments and stir regularly. This will take approximately 45 minutes. The risotto is finished when the buckwheat is tender and the texture is creamy. Stir through the parmesan and season with salt and pepper.

135

The risotto will thicken slightly as it cools. If it becomes too thick, simply stir through a little heated stock or boiling water.

To serve:
Divide the risotto between four bowls. Top with roasted broccoli, a generous sprinkling of pine nuts and a little additional parmesan. Serve immediately.

VEGAN NACHOS
w/ sweet potato chips

Mexican food is always a good idea! My vegan version of nachos boasts a
mega dose of vegetable goodness and is a great shared meal. I've replaced
store-bought fried corn chips with homemade sweet potato chips –
they're divine.

136

SWEET POTATO CHIPS
2 medium **sweet potatoes** – washed
2–3 tablespoons **melted coconut oil**
Salt

VEGAN CHILLI
4 **garlic cloves**
1 **onion** – finely diced
1 large **red chilli** –
de-seeded and finely chopped
1 **carrot** – peeled and diced
1 stem **celery** – sliced thinly
2 **red capsicums** –
trimmed and cut into chunks
1 teaspoon **fennel seeds**
1 tablespoon **ground cumin**
½ teaspoon **hot smoked paprika**
1 teaspoon **garam masala**
¼ teaspoon **ground cinnamon**
250g **brown mushrooms** –
roughly chopped (I use Swiss brown
or Portobello mushrooms)
2 cups (500ml) **vegetable stock**
2 x 400g tins **chopped tomatoes in juice**
1 x 400g can **cannellini beans** –
drained and rinsed
1 x 400g can **black beans** –
drained and rinsed
1 x 400g can **kidney beans** –
drained and rinsed
Handful **fresh coriander** – roughly chopped
Olive oil / coconut oil for sautéing
Salt and **cracked black pepper**

GUACAMOLE
2 **ripe avocados**
Juice of 2 **limes** (or two small lemons)
Handful **fresh coriander** – roughly chopped
Salt and cracked black pepper

Preheat oven to 180°C (350°F).

Slice the kumara very thinly using a mandolin (leave the skin on). Toss with the melted coconut oil. Line two large baking sheets with baking paper. Lay out the chips. Can overlap very slightly, as they will shrink as they cook.

Bake for 10 minutes before flipping. Bake for a further 10 minutes. Keep a close eye on the chips, removing any that start to brown before the rest. Lay out on plates lined with kitchen paper to cool. Sprinkle with sea salt. Once cool you can store in an airtight container until needed.

Heat a generous glug of oil in a large soup pot over a medium heat. Add the garlic, onions, chilli, carrot and celery. Cook for 10 minutes, stirring regularly, until the onion is tender and translucent. Add the capsicum, fennel seeds and spices. Cook for a further 3 minutes.

Add the mushrooms, stock, tomatoes and beans. Bring to a rolling boil before reducing to simmer for 60–70 minutes until thickened. Remove from the heat and stir through the coriander.

Season generously with salt and cracked black pepper.

Mash the avocados until desired consistency is achieved. Stir through the lime juice and coriander. Season generously.

137

4 DF GF V VEG

SWEET POTATO GNOCCHI
w/ broccoli, macadamia & basil pesto

If you've never tried gnocchi before, please give it a go! It's more simple to put together than you might think. The broccoli pesto adds a lovely nutritious touch and is really tasty. This vegetarian dish is a great one to serve up to friends or as a way to convince your children that vegetables are awesome.

The gnocchi can also be made by replacing the sweet potato with parsnip. It's quite a different flavour but is excellent too.

138

Combine all pesto ingredients in a food processor. Blitz until your desired consistency is reached. Season generously.

Preheat oven to 180°C (350°F).

Bake the sweet potato whole for 45–60 minutes until very tender. Cut in half and scoop out soft flesh. Mash until smooth.

Place potatoes in a medium pot of cold water. Boil for 20 minutes until soft. Drain and mash until fairly smooth without adding any liquid.

GNOCCHI

1 large **orange sweet potato** – washed
1 large / 2 medium **potatoes** – peeled and cut into chunks
2 **egg yolks**
½ cup (85g) **white rice flour**
½ cup (60g) **tapioca flour**
¾ teaspoon **sea salt**
Ghee for sautéing

Combine the potato and sweet potato together. Leave to cool. You'll need just two cups of the mash. Place in a large bowl along with the egg, half the white rice flour, half the tapioca flour and the salt. Use a wooden spoon to stir together. Add the remaining flour and use your hands to bring the dough together. It will be quite sticky.

PESTO

¾ cup small **broccoli florets** (raw)
1 tightly packed cup **fresh basil leaves**
½ small clove **garlic** – finely chopped
2 tablespoons **fresh lemon juice**
½ cup (65g) **raw macadamia nuts**
½ cup (125ml) **extra virgin olive oil**
Salt and **cracked black pepper**

Put the dough on a board that is well dusted with rice flour. Form a disc shape and cut into quarters. Cut each quarter in half so that you have 8 pieces of dough.

139

Re-dust the board and roll each piece into a log that is roughly 2cm in width. Cut at 3cm intervals along the log. Repeat this process until all of the dough pieces are used.

TO SERVE

Additional salt and cracked black pepper and basil leaves

Lay raw gnocchi out a large board or plates lined with baking paper.

* You can freeze uncooked gnocchi for up to a month. I cook them straight from the freezer in boiling water. I'll always sauté the cooked gnocchi if they've been previously frozen as they'll have absorbed a bit of extra moisture in the freezing process and can be a bit sticky.

Bring a large pot of well-salted water to the boil. Drop the gnocchi into the water – 12–15 pieces at a time. They will be ready in 1–2 minutes – when they float to the surface. Repeat until you've cooked all the gnocchi*.

Heat a generous dollop of ghee in a large sauté pan over a medium or high heat. Add the gnocchi and cook for a couple of minutes on each side until golden.

Toss gnocchi with the pesto. Divide among plates. Garnish with fresh basil, cracked black pepper and salt. Serve immediately.

MAC 'N' CHEESE
w/ creamy cauliflower sauce

This is HEAVEN! I've created a more nutritious version of the dish that was my childhood favourite (and one of the first things I learnt how to cook). The sauce uses cauliflower to replace the traditional milk-heavy béchamel sauce. There is an entire head of cauliflower hiding in it but all you taste is creamy deliciousness. This is a great dish to serve up to my daughter when she comes home tired from daycare. She loves it and I know it contains some real goodness.

140

1 medium **onion** – finely diced
2 **garlic cloves** – finely diced
1 medium / large head **cauliflower** –
cut into florets
2 cups (500ml) **vegetable / chicken stock**
1½ cups (150g) grated **cheddar cheese**
1 tablespoon **butter**
250g **gluten-free pasta** (penne, spirals or
macaroni all work well)
¾ cup (90g) **gluten-free breadcrumbs**
1 cup (100g) additional grated **cheddar cheese**
for topping
Salt and **cracked black pepper**
Ghee (see page 198) / **coconut oil** for sautéing

Heat a generous dollop of oil in large sauté
pan (one that comes with a lid) over a
medium heat. Add the onion and garlic and
cook for 5 minutes until translucent. Add
the cauliflower and stock. Gently simmer
with the lid on for 15–20 minutes until the
cauliflower is very tender.

Use either a powerful blender or a hand
blender to puree the cauliflower and stock
until silky smooth. Stir through the butter
and cheese. Season to taste with salt and
cracked black pepper.

141

Cook the pasta according to the packet
instructions. Combine the drained pasta with
the cauliflower sauce.

Preheat oven to 200°C (390°F).

Spoon pasta and sauce into an oven-proof
dish. Scatter the breadcrumbs on top,
followed by the additional cheese. Bake for
20–25 minutes until golden brown on top.

Leftover pasta can be stored in the fridge
in an airtight container for up to two days.
Gently reheat in the oven.

TAMARIND & COCONUT LENTILS

This recipe is a cornerstone of my home kitchen and has been for years now. It's simple to make and full of rich and satisfying flavour. I make up a big batch to ensure we've got easy lunches and dinners for the week ahead, and always like to have some portions in the freezer.

Soaking the lentils beforehand ensures easier digestion.
Try not to skip this step.

My favourite accompaniment is cauliflower rice (see page 206) as it stops the meal being too heavy. My daughter Bonnie loves this recipe with steamed millet which has been stirred with a large knob of butter. I serve it topped with a drizzle of coconut cream or yoghurt.

142

2 cups (420g) raw brown lentils
3 tablespoons coconut oil for sautéing
1 onion – finely diced
4 large garlic cloves
3 tablespoons finely grated ginger
1 red chilli – de-seeded and finely chopped
3 tablespoons finely grated turmeric root
or 1 tablespoon ground turmeric
1 tablespoon ground cumin
1 teaspoon garam masala
1 teaspoon fennel seeds
1L vegetable stock
(can also use chicken stock)
2 cups (500ml) water
1 tablespoon tamarind paste
1 x 400g can chopped tomatoes
1 x 400g can coconut cream
Salt and cracked black pepper

Place the lentils in a large bowl and cover with water. Leave to soak for 4–12 hours. Drain and rinse well.

Melt the coconut oil in a large soup pot over a medium heat. Add the onion, garlic, ginger, chilli and fresh turmeric root (if using). Sauté for 5 minutes until the onion is translucent. Add the ground turmeric (if not using fresh), cumin, garam masala and fennel seeds. Cook for 1–2 minutes until fragrant.

143

Add the lentils, stock, water, tamarind and tinned tomatoes. Bring to a boil and then reduce to a rolling simmer. Cook for 45 minutes before adding coconut cream. Simmer for a further 15–20 minutes. Season to taste.

Will last up to four days in an airtight container in the fridge. Can be frozen for up to three months.

CREAMY PARSNIP 'RISOTTO'
w/ mushrooms

Parsnip stands in for rice so very beautifully in this rich and creamy dish.
The result is deeply satisfying without the heaviness of traditional risotto.
You'll need a high-speed blender to chop the parsnip or you can chop it
very finely by hand.

Parsnips and mushrooms are a deliciously earthy combination.

144

5 medium **parsnips**
3 medium **garlic cloves** – finely diced
1 small **onion** / 1 **leek** – finely diced
1½ cups (375ml) **vegetable stock**
1 tablespoon **fresh thyme leaves**
500g Portobello / Swiss brown
mushrooms – sliced
½ cup (125ml) **pouring cream** (could use
additional stock instead to make dairy-free)
Salt and **cracked black pepper**
Ghee (see page 198) / **other oil** for sautéing

TO GARNISH
Fresh thyme leaves
micro-greens (optional)

Peel the parsnips and chop into thick slices. Use a high-speed blender to blitz until a bit larger than a cooked grain of rice – do this in 2–3 batches so that the appliance is able to chop consistently.

Heat a generous spoonful of oil or ghee over a medium heat in a sauté pan. Add the onion or leek and ⅔ of the garlic, sauté gently for 5 minutes until the onion is translucent. Add the parsnip rice. Cook for 4 minutes, moving frequently. Add the stock and thyme. Cook for a further 12 minutes or so, stirring often, until cooked but not mushy.

145

Meanwhile, heat a generous spoonful of oil in another sauté pan over a medium or high heat. Add the mushrooms and remaining garlic. Sauté for 5 minutes until tender.

Add the mushrooms to the parsnip risotto along with the cream. Cook and stir for 2 minutes. If a looser consistency is preferred, more stock or boiling water can be added, ¼ cup at a time. Season generously with salt and cracked black pepper. Serve immediately.

Leftovers will last two days in the fridge. Additional liquid may need to be added when reheating.

SMOKY & SPICY SPANISH BEANS
w/ paprika & saffron

I can absolutely promise there is no chance you will make this dish only once.
The full flavour is pure happiness. Great for feeding a crowd or for stocking
your freezer with meal solutions for busy times. Pair with steamed millet or
thick slices of toasted sourdough. I serve leftovers for brunch sometimes too.
With a fried egg on top, it's a fabulous way to start the day.

146

1 **onion** – finely diced
4 **garlic cloves**– finely diced
2 **carrot** – finely diced
1 teaspoon **cumin seeds**
1 teaspoon **fennel seeds**
2½ cups (625ml) **vegetable stock**
(can also use chicken stock)
2 x 400g cans **cannellini beans** –
drained and rinsed well
1 x 400g can **butter beans** –
drained and rinsed well
2 x 400g cans **cherry tomatoes**
1 **bay leaf** (optional)
2 pinches **saffron threads**
¾ teaspoon **hot-smoked paprika**
1 tablespoon **fresh thyme leaves**
Zest of 1 lemon
Large bunch **kale** (6 leaves) – trimmed of
stalks and cut into thick ribbons
Sea salt and **cracked black pepper**
3 tablespoons **ghee** (see page 198)
or **coconut oil** for sautéing

TO SERVE
Fresh thyme leaves
Slivered almonds (omit if nut-free)

Heat three tablespoons of oil in a large sauté
pan over a medium heat. Add the onion,
garlic and carrot.

Cook gently for 5 minutes until the onion is
translucent and tender. Add the cumin and
fennel seeds and sauté for 1 minute.

Add the stock, beans, tinned tomatoes, bay
leaf, saffron threads, paprika, thyme leaves
and lemon zest. Bring to a boil and then
simmer over a low heat for 60 minutes. Stir
often to ensure not sticking to the bottom of
the pan. Remove bay leaf.

Add the kale and cook for 3 minutes until
just wilted.

Season generously with sea salt and
cracked black pepper.

Leftovers will last up to four days in an
airtight container in the fridge.

Can be frozen for up to two months.

WEEKNIGHT NOODLES

Preparing nutritious weeknight meals can be tough when you are short on time. This simple recipe comes together really fast. I use a good-quality store-bought spice paste (usually of an Indonesian variety) to do all the work. This gives you a robust flavour base to cook your vegetables and egg. We mostly eat this as a meat-free meal but feel free to add a meat protein if you'd prefer.

150g thick **dried rice noodles**
(sometimes called Pad Thai noodles)
1 **onion** – finely diced
1 heaped tablespoon **Penang spice paste**
or **laksa** or **green curry paste**
1 medium head **broccoli** – cut into florets
1 medium **carrot** – peeled, trimmed
and cut into fine ribbons with a mandoline
peeler. Alternatively you can coarsely
grate the carrot.
½ cup (80g) **frozen peas**
2 tablespoons **tamari**
2 large free-range **eggs** – lightly beaten
Handful **fresh coriander** – roughly chopped
Coconut oil / ghee (see page 198) for sautéing

TO SERVE
Sesame seeds (black or white)
Fresh chilli
Additional coriander leaves

Bring a large saucepan of water to the boil. Add the noodles and cook according to the packet instructions. Drain and run under cold water to cool. Set aside until needed.

Heat a generous dollop of oil in a sauté pan over a medium heat. Add the onion and cook gently for 4–5 minutes until translucent. Add the spice paste and carrot. Cook for 1 minute. Add the broccoli and peas. Raise heat to high. Cook for 4 minutes. Toss through the noodles and the tamari. Add a couple of tablespoons of water or coconut cream if the pan is too dry. Reduce heat to medium and push vegetables to one side of the pan. Add a small dollop of oil and then pour the eggs in the open space. Let sit for a minute to firm up on the bottom before mixing through the noodles for a further minute. Sprinkle with coriander leaves.

Taste and add additional tamari if you wish.

Divide between bowls. Garnish \with additional coriander, chilli and sesame seeds.

148

ZUCCHINI NOODLE RAMEN
w/ miso-roasted eggplant
& perfect soft-boiled eggs

Many of my preferred meals are broth-based. They feel so deeply nourishing.
When the chill of a winter's day has entered my bones and refuses to budge,
a big bowl of vegetables and broth will chase it away every time. I have
replaced traditional wheat noodles with zucchini 'noodles' here. They make
this a lighter meal and deliver a hearty dose of green goodness.

150

1 **eggplant** – cut into 3 cm chunks
3 tablespoons **oil** for roasting
2 free-range **eggs**

MISO MARINADE
2 tablespoons **white miso paste**
½ teaspoon **rice wine vinegar**
1 teaspoon **tamari**
1 teaspoon **maple syrup / rice malt syrup**
1 tablespoon **olive oil**
1 tablespoon **water**

RAMEN STOCK & VEGETABLES
3 cups (750ml) good-quality **vegetable stock**
(can also use Chicken Bone Broth {see page 214})
1 teaspoon finely grated **ginger**
2 teaspoons **rice wine vinegar**
2 teaspoons **tamari**
½ head **broccoli** – cut into florets
1 medium **carrot** –
cut into ribbons using a julienne peeler
1 **spring onion** – sliced
4 **button mushrooms** sliced
3 **zucchini** – trimmed and cut into 'noodles' using
a spiraliser

TO SERVE
Additional sliced spring onion
Black and white sesame seeds

To make the marinade:
Whisk together the miso paste, rice wine vinegar, tamari, maple syrup, oil and water until smooth.

Preheat oven to 180°C (350°F). Toss the eggplant with three tablespoons of oil and bake for 30 minutes, flipping at least once. Toss with the miso marinade and roast for a further 15 minutes. Keep warm until ready to use.

Lower the eggs into a saucepan of boiling water and cook for 5 minutes (small or medium sized egg) or 6 minutes (large egg). Run the eggs under cold water before peeling. Set aside until assembling the dish.

To make the stock and vegetables:
Combine the vegetable stock, ginger, rice wine vinegar and tamari. Simmer for 4 minutes. Add the spring onion, broccoli, carrot and mushrooms and cook for a further 4 minutes.

Put the zucchini 'noodles' into the hot stock for 1 minute before removing the saucepan from the heat. Divide the vegetables and noodles between two bowls. Cut the eggs in half and place on top. Add the eggplant and serve immediately.

151

CREAMY LEEK, CHARD
& tarragon tart
w/ buckwheat & brown rice crust

This greedily-stuffed tart is pure pleasure to eat. If you've never made gluten-free pastry from scratch because it felt too intimidating, you'll find this method really straight forward. I love the anise flavour of tarragon partnered with the creamy egg centre. Serve with a crisp salad. This tart really sings, whether you have it for lunch or dinner, hot or cold.

152

PASTRY
½ cup (65g) **buckwheat flour**
½ cup (60g) **tapioca flour**
1 cup (140g) **brown rice flour**
75g **cold butter** – cut into cubes
1 free-range **egg**
¼ teaspoon **sea salt**
1–4 tablespoons **cold water**
(only added as needed)

FILLING
2 small **leeks** – white part sliced into rings
(Use 1½ if only large leeks available)
2 large **garlic cloves** – finely diced
6 free-range **eggs** – lightly beaten
¼ cup **cream**
1 cup (100g) grated **cheddar cheese**
½ teaspoon **dried tarragon**
2 leaves **Swiss chard / silver beet** –
stems removed and torn into chunks
Oil for roasting and sautéing
Salt and **cracked black pepper**

Combine all pastry ingredients (except water) in a food processor and run until the texture of coarse breadcrumbs. Add the water one tablespoon at a time –leaving five seconds between each addition – until the pastry comes together in a ball. Shape into a thick disc, wrap in cling film and place in the fridge for a minimum of 30 minutes and up to 24 hours.

Preheat oven to 180°C (350°F). Remove the pastry from fridge and roll out on a floured board until slightly less than 1cm thick. Drape over a 20cm round tart dish and gently press into the tin. Use a knife to trim the top edge. Bake for 12–15 minutes (using pastry weights if you have them) until firm and very slightly golden. Set aside to cool.

Heat a generous dollop of oil in a sauté pan over a medium heat. Add the leek and garlic. Cook gently for 10 minutes without browning, adding the tarragon in the last 3 minutes of cooking. Leave to cool for 15 minutes.

Combine the eggs, cream and cheese in a bowl, season generously and whisk well. Pour into the cooled pastry shell. Scatter the torn chard leaves and press under the liquid. Spread the leek and garlic mixture across the top.

Bake at 180°C (350°F) for 30–35 minutes until just firm in the centre. Do not overcook. Leave to sit for 15 minutes before cutting. Serve with a crisp salad.

Leftovers can be stored in an airtight container in the fridge for up to three days.

153

SWEET

Roasted rhubarb w/ quinoa shortbread crumble	156 — GF VEG
Rustic pear galette w/ walnut pastry	158 — GF VEG
Chocolate chia mousse	160 — DF GF NF GRFR VEGN
Blueberry, dark chocolate & molasses brownie	162 — DF GF VEG GRFR
Fresh berry clafoutis	164 — GF VEG
Raw chocolate bark w/ pistachios & goji berries	166 — DF GF GRFR VEGN
Coco-nutty shortbread cookies	166 — DF VEG
Coconut & lemon tapioca pudding	168 — DF GF GRFR VEGN
Banana coconut breakfast cake	170 — DF GF VEG NF
Matcha & spirulina energy bars	172 — DF GF VEGN
Fool-proof gluten free chocolate cake	174 — GF VEG GRFR
Almond butter & vanilla crunch	176 — DF GF VEGN
Salted chocolate & rosemary tart w/ almond & macadamia crust	178 — GF VEG GRFR
Peanut butter & chocolate chunk cookies	180 — DF GF
Zucchini, carrot & banana loaf	182 — DF GF VEG NF
My favourite flavoured nut & seed milks (strawberry cashew / vanilla walnut / cacao pumpkin seed)	184 — DF GF GRFR VEGN
Green tea & vanilla bean panna cotta	186 — GF NF GRFR
Mango & coconut ice blocks w/ raw cacao dip & bee pollen	188 — DF GF NF GRFR VEGN
Coconut & vanilla custard	190 — DF GF VEG
Grain-free carrot, hazlenut & lemon babycakes	192 — GF VEG GRFR
Baby banana pikelets	194 — DF GF VEG NF

155

ROASTED RHUBARB
w/ quinoa shortbread crumble

My household goes crazy for crumble. It's one of our most-loved desserts, and enjoying the leftovers for breakfast might be even better. Rhubarb from my mother-in-law's garden is our top pick for fruit. Its tart tang and beautiful colour are hard to resist. The crumble has the texture of delicate shortbread with a pleasant earthiness from the quinoa flour.

156

10 stalks **rhubarb** – leaves removed
Juice of 1 **orange**
1 teaspoon good-quality **vanilla extract**
2 tablespoons **coconut sugar**

CRUMBLE TOPPING
¾ cup (75g) **quinoa flakes**
½ cup (60g) **tapioca flour**
100g **cold butter** – cut into cubes
¼ cup (50g) **coconut sugar**
or **light muscovado sugar**
2 teaspoons good-quality **vanilla extract**

TO SERVE
Cream, vanilla ice cream
or thick Greek yoghurt

Preheat oven to 180°C (350°F).

Cut rhubarb into 5cm pieces. Toss with the orange juice and vanilla.

Place fruit in an ovenproof dish, sprinkle with sugar, cover loosely with foil and roast for 30–35 minutes until it's tender but still retaining its shape.

Combine all crumble ingredients in a large bowl. Use your hands to rub the butter into the flours until the mixture is the texture of coarse breadcrumbs. You can also use a food processor for this step, which makes the process very speedy.

Place the roasted fruit in a 22cm round ovenproof skillet or dish. Scatter the crumble evenly over the top.

Bake for 30–35 minutes uncovered until lightly golden. Let stand for 10 minutes before serving.

Pair with cream, vanilla ice cream or thick Greek yoghurt.

RUSTIC PEAR GALETTE
w/ walnut pastry

I adore the rustic beauty of a handmade tart. Sweet pears and the wonderful
earthy flavour of walnuts make this a dreamy dessert. The pastry, when
uncooked is delicate so handle with care. Serve warm with organic cream.

158

PASTRY
1 cup (100g) roughly chopped **walnuts**
¾ cup (105g) **brown rice flour**
½ cup (60g) **tapioca flour**
50g **cold butter** – cut into cubes
¼ cup (50g) **coconut sugar**
or **light muscovado sugar**
1 free-range **egg**
1–2 tablespoons **cold water** (if necessary)

FRUIT FILLING
3 medium **pears** – peeled and cored
3 tablespoons **maple syrup**
4 teaspoons **tapioca flour**
Juice of ½ **lemon**

To make the pastry:
Place walnuts into a food processor and blitz until the consistency of coarse breadcrumbs. Add the tapioca flour, brown rice flour, butter, sugar and egg. Run for a minute until this mixture too has the texture of coarse breadcrumbs. Add the water one tablespoon at a time, leaving five seconds between each addition, until the dough comes together in a ball.

Wrap in cling-film and place in the fridge for at least 30 minutes and up to one day.

Slice the pears and place in a bowl with the lemon juice and maple syrup. Sprinkle with the tapioca flour and, using your hands, gently mix through, ensuring the fruit is evenly coated.

Preheat oven to 180°C (350°F).

Take the dough from the fridge and place on a large piece of baking paper. Roll out until roughly circular and approximately 40cm in diameter. If the dough is quite sticky, roll out between two sheets of baking paper.

Tile the pears on top of pastry, leaving 5cm around the edge. Place your hands under the baking paper the pastry is laid on and fold the pastry over the fruit. It doesn't need to be perfect. Tidy up any cracks in the pastry if necessary.

Bake for 40 minutes until the pears are tender and the pastry is golden.

Let sit for 20 minutes before serving.

159

6 DF GF NF GRFR VEGN

CHOCOLATE CHIA MOUSSE

This simple blend of ingredients makes the most incredible dessert. At once decadent and healthy, this mousse will well and truly satisfy your chocolate cravings. Use a high-powered blender for the silkiest mousse possible but good results will still be achieved with a regular blender.

I like to top the mousse with freeze-dried raspberries, edible flowers, fresh berries, fresh figs or dark chocolate shavings.

160

400ml coconut cream
⅓ cup (50g) chia seeds
¼ cup (60ml) pure maple syrup / raw honey
3 tablespoons raw cacao powder
1 teaspoon good-quality vanilla essence
Pinch salt

Combine ingredients in a blender (preferably a powerful one) and blitz for 3–4 minutes (or longer) until the mix is as silky smooth as possible. Refrigerate for at least one hour until chilled and firm.

Will last three days in an airtight container in the fridge.

— WHOLEHEARTED: INSPIRING REAL FOOD FOR EVERY DAY —

BLUEBERRY, DARK CHOCOLATE
& molasses brownie

The deep, dark richness of molasses is utterly divine with chocolate, while bursts of fruity sweetness from fresh blueberries add a soft balance. I adore these brownies as a dessert with a generous pour of cream, or as an afternoon treat with a mug of tea. ALWAYS a crowd pleaser.

5 free-range **eggs** – lightly beaten
½ cup (100g) **coconut sugar**
or **light muscovado sugar**
2 tablespoons **blackstrap molasses**
1 teaspoon good-quality **vanilla essence**
¼ cup (60ml) melted **coconut oil**
(can also use butter)
1½ cups (165g) **almond meal / ground almonds**
6 tablespoons good-quality **dark cocoa powder**
or **cacao powder**
½ cup (60g) **tapioca flour**
1 teaspoon **gluten-free baking powder**
1½ cups (225g) **fresh / frozen blueberries**
¾ cup (120g) **dark chocolate chips**

Preheat oven to 180°C (350°F)

Combine the eggs, vanilla, molasses and sugar in a large bowl. Whisk for 3 minutes. Add almond meal and melted oil and stir until well combined.

Sift in cocoa, tapioca flour and baking powder and mix well.

Gently fold in the chocolate chips and half the blueberries. Pour into a lined slice tin. Sprinkle over the remaining blueberries and gently press into the batter until half submerged.

Bake in a 30cm x 12cm tin for about 25 minutes until just cooked. Allow the brownies to cool for 30 minutes before slicing and serving.

Can be stored in the fridge for up to four days or frozen for up to a month.

FRESH BERRY CLAFOUTIS

Luscious and deeply comforting, clafoutis may well be my all-time favourite dessert. This French flan satisfies all my custard desires as well as having a divine crust – it's pretty much perfect. Very quick to pull together – great when you need to make something beautiful in a pinch.

Traditionally it is made with cherries. I favour a mix of fresh berries when they are in season.

164

¾ cup (85g) **almond meal**
2 tablespoons **white rice flour**
3 tablespoons **tapioca flour**
4 large free-range **eggs**
1½ teaspoons good-quality **vanilla essence**
or **seeds** from 1 **vanilla pod**
150ml **pouring cream**
150ml **full-fat milk**
½ cup (100g) **coconut / light muscovado sugar**
1½ cups (225g) **fresh berries**
(blueberries, raspberries and blackberries are my favourites)

Preheat oven to 180°C (350°F).

Combine all ingredients (except fruit) in a large bowl and whisk until well mixed.

Pour into a well-greased 25cm round ovenproof dish. Distribute the fruit over the top. Bake for 35–40 minutes until lightly golden and just set in the centre.

Serve with cream or ice-cream.

RAW CHOCOLATE BARK
w/ pistachios & goji berries

I love the dark bitterness of this simple raw chocolate. I've been known to eat a piece for breakfast. It's only lightly sweetened, with a pleasing crunch from the nuts and a delicious chewiness from the goji berries.

¾ cup (185ml) **organic cold-pressed coconut oil**
¼ cup (60ml) **pure maple syrup**
¾ cup (90g) **raw cacao powder**
1 teaspoon good-quality **vanilla essence**
Pinch **salt**
¼ cup (30g) **goji berries**
½ cup (70g) **pistachio nuts** – roughly chopped

Place the coconut oil in a saucepan over a very low heat. Remove as soon as the oil is almost liquid. Add the maple syrup, raw cacao powder, salt and vanilla. Whisk until smooth. Pour into a small slice tin lined with baking paper. Sprinkle with goji berries and pistachios. Place in the freezer for two hours to set before breaking into pieces. Must be stored in the freezer in an airtight container. Will last up to two months.

166

(leaf) GF   (v) VEG

COCO-NUTTY SHORTBREAD COOKIES

With the buttery richness of shortbread and a pleasing crispness, these cookies are definite winners – I hope you'll love them as much we do. A happy afternoon is me settled in with a cup of tea and a couple of these. Bonnie is always overjoyed when they appear in her lunchbox. These cookies will freeze well so you could make a double batch and have them on hand for ages.

Makes 15-18 cookies

¾ cup (75g) **quinoa flakes**
¾ cup (90g) **tapioca flour**
¾ cup (75g) **desiccated coconut**
½ teaspoon **baking soda**
75g room-temperature **butter** – cut into cubes
3 rounded tablespoons **rice malt syrup** or **maple syrup**

Preheat oven to 180°C (350°F).

Combine all ingredients in a food processor and run until thoroughly mixed.

Dollop rounded teaspoons of batter onto a lined baking sheet. Use damp fingers to lightly press down.

Bake for 20–25 minutes until very lightly golden. Wait 20 minutes before moving from the tray, as they are fragile until cooled.

COCONUT & LEMON
tapioca pudding

Tapioca is a pure delight as dessert. The texture is pleasing and the rich vanilla and coconut flavour glorious. Wholesome enough for an everyday treat and beautiful when prettied up with tropical fruit to serve at a dinner party.

168

½ cup (90g) **tapioca pearls**
2 cups (500ml) **almond milk**
1 cup (250ml) **full-fat coconut cream**
1 teaspoon good-quality **vanilla essence**
or **seeds** from 1 **vanilla pod**
3 tablespoons **coconut sugar**
Finely grated **zest** of 1 large **lemon**
1 **mango** – peeled and cut into small cubes

TO GARNISH
Black sesame seeds

Soak tapioca in one cup of the almond milk for 4–8 hours. Place the soaked tapioca and remaining almond milk in a saucepan with all the remaining ingredients except the mango. Bring to a boil and simmer for 12–15 minutes, stirring continuously until the tapioca is tender.

Place in the fridge to cool for at least three hours. If the pudding has thickened too much, you can create a softer texture by stirring through a little extra almond milk or coconut cream.

To serve:
Divide tapioca between glasses or small dishes. Spoon mango over the top and sprinkle with black sesame seeds.

Leftover tapioca pudding will last in an airtight container in the fridge for up to three days.

BANANA COCONUT BREAKFAST CAKE

A version of this cake has been the most viewed recipe on my blog since it was posted a few years ago. The name came about because it is made with such simple ingredients (and so little sugar) that it is wholesome enough to eat for breakfast. It is nut-, dairy- and gluten-free, making it an excellent choice for kids' lunchboxes.

170

2 very **ripe bananas** – lightly mashed
½ cup (125ml) **coconut cream**
(can also use yoghurt)
1 teaspoon good-quality **vanilla extract**
4 free-range **eggs**
1¼ cups (125g) **desiccated coconut**
¼ cup (30g) **coconut flour**
½ cup (70g) **brown rice flour / spelt flour**
¾ teaspoon **baking soda**
1 teaspoon **apple cider vinegar**

TO GARNISH
Coconut chips (optional)

Preheat oven to 180°C (350°F).

Put the banana, coconut cream, vanilla and eggs into a food processor and process until smooth. Add the remaining ingredients and run for a minute until well mixed. Leave batter to sit for 10 minutes to allow the coconut flour to absorb the moisture. Process briefly again before pouring into a 21cm spring-form cake tin lined with baking paper. Place the cake on a flat surface and wiggle lightly to flatten the top. Sprinkle with coconut chips if using.

Bake for 50–55 minutes until golden and a skewer comes out clean when inserted.

Leave to cool for 30 minutes before cutting.

Store in the fridge in an airtight container for up to four days.

MATCHA & SPIRULINA ENERGY BARS

I've paired my two favorite green powders to make snack bars full of healthy fats and appealing flavours. This is happy snacking.

Makes 12-16 bars

172

1½ cups (225g) **raw almonds**
5 tablespoons (40g) **chia seeds**
1 cup (30g) **unsweetened puffed rice / millet**
¼ cup (40g) **sesame seeds**
¼ cup (35g) **raw pumpkin seeds**
¼ cup (35g) **raw sunflower seeds**
1 cup (80g) **coconut threads**
1 tablespoon **matcha powder**
1 heaped teaspoon **spirulina powder**
⅓ cup (80ml) **rice malt syrup** (can also use maple syrup but will be sweeter)
1 teaspoon good-quality **vanilla extract**

Preheat oven to 170°C (340°F).

Place the almonds in a food processor or blender and blitz until the texture of coarse breadcrumbs.

Add to other dry ingredients (including matcha and spirulina) and mix in a large bowl.

Combine the rice malt syrup and vanilla in a small saucepan and place over a low heat until runny. Pour the liquid over the dry ingredients and fold through well with a large spoon or spatula.

Firmly press the mixture into a small slice tin (measuring 12cm x 30cm) lined with baking paper. Dampen your hands slightly if the mixture is too sticky.

Use the back of a spoon to smooth out the top.

Bake for 35 minutes until lightly golden. Cool completely before cutting.

Store in the fridge in an airtight container for up to a week. Freezes well.

FOOLPROOF GLUTEN-FREE
chocolate cake

Everyone needs a chocolate cake recipe they can rely on. This is mine. It comes together really quickly in a food processor. The crumb is soft because of the almond meal and has a fudgy denseness from the addition of dates as sweetener. I love to pile the cake high with vanilla-spiked mascarpone instead of a chocolate frosting as I think the colour contrast is divine and the creaminess pairs perfectly. A dark chocolate ganache would work beautifully too.

The cake actually gets better a day or so after baking so feel free to make it 24–48 hours before you'll be serving it.

174

1½ cups (255g) **dried dates**
¼ cup (60ml) melted **coconut oil**
1 teaspoon good-quality **vanilla essence**
5 tablespoons good-quality **dark cocoa**
1 teaspoon **gluten-free baking powder**
6 free-range **eggs** – lightly beaten
2 ½ cups (275g) **almond meal**
100g **dark chocolate** – roughly chopped

TOPPING
400g **mascarpone cheese**
1 tablespoon **maple syrup**
½ teaspoon **vanilla powder**
or **seeds** from 1 **vanilla pod**

TO GARNISH
Flowers
Roughly chopped dark chocolate

Preheat oven to 165°C (330°F).

Place dates in a large bowl and cover with boiling water. Leave to soak for 10 minutes before draining well. Place in a food processor along with the coconut oil and vanilla. Blitz to a coarse paste. Add the cocoa powder, baking powder and eggs. Process for 1 minute until well mixed. Add almond meal and run until combined.

Use a spatula to transfer the cake batter to a large bowl. Fold through the dark chocolate.

Pour the cake batter into a 22cm spring-form cake tin lined with baking paper. Wiggle the tin on the bench top to flatten the surface of the batter.

Bake for 50–55 minutes until a skewer comes out clean when inserted. Leave to cool for 30 minutes before removing from the tin, and place in fridge for one hour to cool before adding the topping.

To make the topping:
Mix the mascarpone cheese, maple syrup and vanilla powder together in a large bowl. Pile on top of the cake, using a palate knife or wide knife to distribute evenly. It does not have to look perfect. Part of the charm of this cake is its rustic appearance.

Garnish with flowers and additional chopped chocolate.

The cake will last up to four days in the fridge.

— KELLY GIBNEY —

ALMOND BUTTER & VANILLA CRUNCH

My daughter Bonnies LOVES this slice. The crunchy texture is a hit with kids generally. Great for lunchboxes and parties. Use rice malt syrup because it provides the necessary binding properties without the intense sweetness of maple syrup or honey.

Makes 12-16 slices

176

½ cup (120g) **almond butter** (see page 202)
½ cup (125ml) **rice malt syrup**
1 rounded tablespoon **coconut oil**
1½ teaspoons good-quality **vanilla essence**
3 cups (90g) **unsweetened puffed rice**
¾ cup (75g) **desiccated coconut**
2 tablespoons **chia seeds**

Place the almond butter, rice malt syrup and coconut oil in a small saucepan over a low heat until runny. Do not allow to simmer or bubble.

Put the puffed rice, coconut and chia seeds in a large bowl. Stir to combine. Pour over the warm liquid and mix until evenly coated.

Spoon into a small slice tin lined with baking paper. You may not need to use all of the tin. Aim for your slice to be roughly 3cm high. Compact the mixture with your hands.

Place in the fridge to set for two hours. Cut into 12 slices before serving.

Will need to be stored in the fridge in warmer months.

10 GF V VEG GRFR

SALTED CHOCOLATE & ROSEMARY TART
w/ almond & macadamia crust

This is the perfect dessert to make when you want to really impress guests. The herbaceous flavour of the rosemary is subtle and partners beautifully with the dark chocolate ganache filling. The recipe is much more straightforward than it looks and can be made over a couple of days if you wish.

178

ALMOND & MACADAMIA TART CASE

1 cup (170g) dried dates – soaked in boiling
water for 10 minutes, then drained well
2 cups (220g) almond meal
1 cup (125g) raw macadamia nuts
¼ teaspoon nutmeg
Zest of 1 lemon
1 teaspoon good-quality vanilla essence
1 tablespoon room temperature butter
Pinch salt

TART FILLING

375g dark chocolate – no more than
72% cocoa content
350ml cream
2 x 15cm fresh rosemary stems
Flaky sea salt for serving

To make the base:
Preheat oven to 165c (330°F).

Place the almond meal and macadamia nuts
into a food processor and process until the
blend is a fine crumb. Add the dates and
remaining ingredients and process until the
dates are well blended and the mixture is
sticky and fairly consistent in texture. This
may take a minute or two and you will need
to scrape down the sides occasionally.

Press the mixture into a well-greased
10cm x 35cm rectangular tart tin. Spend
a few minutes doing this. Try to make it as
even in thickness as possible. Use a knife to
tidy the top edge.

Use a piece of baking paper larger than
the tin to lie over the crust, and anchor
with pastry weights, uncooked rice or dried
beans. This "blind baking" stops the crust
rising and cracking as it bakes. Cook for
approximately 15 minutes until golden.
Watch carefully as nut crust can burn easily.
Set aside to cool completely before filling.

179

To make the filling:
Melt the chocolate gently in a metal bowl
or pot over simmering water. Do not let the
chocolate bowl touch the water. Remove
from the heat as soon as the chocolate is
melted. It is better to still have a few bits of
chocolate left (that will gently melt as you
mix) than for the chocolate to overheat
and split.

While you are melting the chocolate, place
the rosemary and cream in a saucepan and
bring to the boil. Stir a few times while it is
heating to help release the rosemary flavour.
Take off the heat as soon as it starts to boil.

Pour the cream through a sieve (to lift out
the rosemary leaves) and into the melted
chocolate. Mix until silky smooth. Pour into
the tart shell (you may not need all the filling
if you use a different size tin).

Set in the fridge for at least three hours.

Remove 30 minutes before serving. Sprinkle
with flaky sea salt and serve with softly
whipped cream.

PEANUT BUTTER
& chocolate chunk cookies

Peanut butter cookies, in my opinion, are up there with some of the best treats around. The combination of slightly salty, chunky peanut butter and shards of roughly chopped dark chocolate is a heady pleasure. I make a batch and then store them in the freezer. They can be eaten immediately after taking them from the freezer, and it means we don't race to eat the whole lot at once.

Makes 18-22 cookies

180

Preheat oven to 180°C (350°F).

Combine all ingredients (except chocolate) in a food processor. Blitz for a minute or two until well mixed. The dough will be very sticky and you'll need to stop to scrape the sides several times.

1 cup (240g) **chunky peanut butter** (I use a good-quality natural peanut butter)
¼ cup (60ml) **pure maple syrup**
½ cup (60g) **tapioca flour**
½ cup (55g) **almond meal** or **ground almonds**
1 teaspoon good-quality **vanilla essence**
2 tablespoons **melted coconut oil** (can also use butter)
2 tablespoons **warm water**
½ cup (60g) roughly chopped **dark chocolate** (I use a 72% dark chocolate)

Transfer the dough to a large bowl and mix the chocolate through, using your hands.

Form tablespoons of the mixture into balls and place on a lined cookie sheet. Use your fingers to press the cookies down. The biscuits mostly hold their shape while cooking so make as flat as you want the end result to be. If the cookie cracks or crumbles while you're doing this, simply reshape it and press it down again.

181

Bake for 15–18 minutes until the cookies are lightly golden. Do not move from the tray for 30 minutes, as they are very fragile until cooled.

Cookies will last up to four days in an airtight container, and can be frozen for a maximum of three months.

ZUCCHINI, CARROT & BANANA LOAF

A lightly sweet loaf with a soft banana flavour, beautifully flecked with the goodness of carrots and zucchini. You'll find me curled up with a thick slice and a mug of tea on slow, lazy mornings. And I've created this to be nut-, gluten- and dairy- free, making it ideal for inclusion in children's lunchboxes.

182

1 very **ripe banana** –
spotty and brown is good!
4 free-range **eggs** – lightly beaten
1 teaspoon good-quality **vanilla essence**
¼ cup (60ml) **rice malt syrup**
or **pure maple syrup**
¼ teaspoon **cinnamon**
1 cup (100g) **desiccated coconut**
1 cup (140g) **brown rice flour**
½ cup (60g) **tapioca flour**
¾ teaspoon **baking soda**
1 teaspoon **apple cider vinegar**
1 cup (100g) grated **carrot** –
tightly squeeze to remove liquid
1 large **zucchini** –
grated and tightly squeezed to remove liquid

Preheat oven to 180°C (350°F).

Mash banana thoroughly and combine in a large bowl with eggs, vanilla and rice malt syrup. Stir until thoroughly mixed. Add the cinnamon, coconut, brown rice flour, tapioca flour, baking soda and apple cider vinegar. Stir well. Add carrot and zucchini. Fold through gently.

Pour batter into a well-greased 23cm loaf tin. Bake for 60–65 minutes until a skewer comes out clean when inserted.

Allow to cool completely before slicing.

MY FAVOURITE FLAVOURED
nut & seed milks

The possibilities are endless when you explore making milk with nuts and
seeds. I choose a different base nut or seed depending on the use
(or my mood!). While almond and coconut milk are probably the most popular
choices around, there are loads of other alternatives. These are my favourites.

Store in an airtight glass vessel in the fridge for up to three days. Will naturally
separate so shake gently before serving.

Makes 750ml

Strawberry Cashew Milk

¾ cups (105g) raw cashew nuts – soaked for 4–6 hours, drained and rinsed.
3 cups (750ml) water
1 teaspoon good-quality vanilla essence
3 tablespoons pure maple syrup or rice malt syrup or raw honey
4 tablespoons freeze-dried strawberry powder (available from specialty food stores)
Pinch salt
2 tablespoons beetroot juice (for more intense colour – optional)

Place the cashew nuts and water in a blender. Blitz until the nuts are very fine. Use a nut-milk bag or piece of muslin to strain the milk into a jug. Squeeze the pulp tightly to extract every bit of liquid possible.

Rinse blender and pour in the strained nut milk. Add the remaining ingredients and process to mix well.

Vanilla Walnut Milk

¾ cup (75g) raw walnuts – soaked for 12–15 hours, drained and rinsed
2–3 tablespoons pure maple syrup (depending on sweetness desired)
3 cups (750ml) water
1 teaspoon vanilla paste or seeds from 1 vanilla pod
(choose good-quality for the best flavour)
Pinch salt

Place the walnuts and water in a blender. Blitz until the nuts are very fine.

Use a nut-milk bag or piece of muslin to strain the milk into a jug. Squeeze the pulp tightly to extract every bit of liquid possible.

Rinse blender and pour in the strained milk. Add the remaining ingredients and process to mix well.

185

Cacao Pumpkin Seed Milk

¾ cup (100g) raw pumpkin seeds – soaked for 12–15 hours, drained and rinsed
3 cups (750ml) water
1 teaspoon good-quality vanilla essence
4 teaspoons raw cacao powder or good-quality dark cocoa
3 tablespoons pure maple syrup or rice malt syrup or raw honey
Pinch salt

Place the pumpkin seeds and water in a blender. Blitz until the seeds are very fine.

Use a nut-milk bag or piece of muslin to strain the milk into a jug. Squeeze the pulp tightly to extract every bit of liquid possible.

Rinse blender and pour in the strained milk. Add the remaining ingredients and process to mix well.

GREEN TEA & VANILLA BEAN
panna cotta

Panna cotta is heaven. Incredibly rich yet light, this dessert feels pretty darn fancy but is very easy to put together. Honestly, the trickiest part is persuading the delicate custards out of the moulds – and I've given you a couple of ways to do this. Perfect for entertaining as they can be made in advance.

The pairing of green tea and vanilla is special. The two flavours play so beautifully. Splurge on a good-quality vanilla. It will make a big difference.

186

2½ gold leaf **gelatin sheets** (5.75g)
350ml **single cream**
150ml **full fat milk**
6 **green tea teabags**
Seeds from 1 **vanilla pod**
or 1 teaspoon good-quality **vanilla paste**
¼ cup (50g) **light muscovado sugar**

TO SERVE
Good-quality dark chocolate – chopped
roughly into shards

Soak the gelatin leaves in a bowl of cold water for 10–15 minutes to soften.

Place the cream, milk, tea bags and vanilla in a saucepan and place over a medium heat for 5 minutes until almost at a boil. Remove from the heat and take out the teabags. Gently squeeze to extract as much flavour as possible.

Stir in the muscovado sugar.

Squeeze the water from the soaked gelatin leaves. Whisk gelatin rapidly into the cream mixture.

Lightly grease four 125ml panna cotta moulds with a mild tasting oil. Pour the hot liquid into the moulds. You can use small dishes or teacups instead. Place into the fridge to set for at least four hours.

To remove the panna cotta, slide a thin knife down to the bottom of the mould, holding it tightly against the edge, to break the vacuum. Turn mould upside down on the plate and shake gently to release. You can also dip the bottom of the mould into hot water for a moment to loosen. Don't do this for too long or the dessert will start to melt.

Sprinkle the panna cotta with dark chocolate shards and serve immediately.

187

MANGO & COCONUT ICE BLOCKS
w/ raw cacao dip & bee pollen

Homemade popsicles are simple to make and give you the opportunity to create a little magic. My daughter really loves bee pollen. It's like fairy dust to her. She was so delighted to see the pretty speckles dot these icy treats.

Makes 6 ice blocks

ICE-BLOCK
1 large **mango** – peeled and roughly chopped
1¼ cups (310ml) **coconut cream**
1 tablespoon **raw honey**
1 teaspoon good-quality **vanilla extract**
¼ teaspoon **ground cinnamon**

CACAO DIP
½ cup (100g) **coconut oil**
¼ cup (30g) **raw cacao powder**
or good-quality **cocoa powder**
¼ cup (75g) **raw honey**
or **pure maple syrup** or **rice malt syrup**

TO GARNISH
2 tablespoons bee pollen

To make the ice-block:
Combine the ice-block ingredients in a blender and blitz until smooth. Pour into ice-block moulds and place in the freezer until solid.

To make the cacao dip:
Combine the coconut oil, cacao powder and honey in a small saucepan over a very low heat. As soon as the oil is mostly liquid, remove from the heat and whisk until smooth. Pour into a small jug that is large enough in which to dip the ice-blocks.

Remove the ice-blocks from the moulds and dip into the raw chocolate. You can dip half as I have done or the entire ice-block. Sprinkle with bee pollen while still wet. Place on a tray or large plate lined with baking paper. Return to the freezer to harden.

Ice-blocks are best stored in an airtight container in the freezer. Put layers of baking paper between the ice-blocks if you are stacking them. They will last a month stored this way.

4 DF GF v VEG

COCONUT & VANILLA CUSTARD

This rich dairy-free custard has the goodness of egg yolks and flecks of real vanilla. Lovely drizzled over stewed fruit, with my pear and walnut galette (see page 158), or even at breakfast with my banana and nutmeg baked oatmeal (see page 40).

2 tablespoons **cornstarch**
1½ cup (325ml) **coconut cream**
1 cup (250ml) **almond milk**
1 teaspoon **vanilla paste**
or **seeds** from 1 **vanilla pod**
3 free-range **egg yolks**
3 tablespoons **maple syrup / rice malt syrup**

Whisk together the cornstarch with a small amount of coconut cream until smooth. Add to a medium saucepan along with rest of the coconut cream, almond milk and vanilla. Cook for 5 minutes, whisking often over a medium or low heat. The mixture may have tiny bubbles around the edge of the pot but do not allow to boil or simmer heavily as this will split the custard.

Combine the egg yolks with three tablespoons of warmed milk in a small dish and whisk. This will ensure the egg yolks can be added to the saucepan without scrambling.

Pour into the saucepan and whisk vigorously. Continue stirring for 5 minutes over the heat, avoiding boiling, until the custard is thick and smooth. Set aside to cool for 15 minutes before serving.

Cold custard will last two days in an airtight container in the fridge and can be gently reheated on the stove over a low heat.

190

GRAIN-FREE CARROT, HAZELNUT
& lemon babycakes

With a warm spiciness and gentle sweetness, these little cakes are great for morning and afternoon tea as well as for celebrations. There may seem to be quite a few ingredients but the whole process is very straightforward.

Makes 12 babycakes

192

100g room-temperature **butter** –
cut into cubes
½ cup (100g) **coconut sugar**
or **light muscovado sugar**
1 **ripe banana** – lightly mashed
5 free-range **eggs**
Zest of 2 **lemons**
1 teaspoon good-quality **vanilla essence**
1 rounded teaspoon **gluten-free baking powder**
1 teaspoon **ground ginger**
1½ teaspoons **ground cinnamon**
¼ teaspoon **ground nutmeg**
½ teaspoon **ground cardamom**
2 cups (220g) **hazelnut meal**
1 cup (110g) **almond meal**
½ cup (50g) **desiccated coconut**
1½ cups (140g) grated **carrot**
¾ cup (95g) **sultanas / raisins**

TOPPING
250g **plain cream cheese**
25g room-temperature **butter** – cut into cubes
½ teaspoon **vanilla powder**
or **seeds** from 1 **vanilla pod**
1 rounded tablespoon **honey**

Preheat oven to 170°C (335°F).

Place the butter and sugar in a food
processor and run until creamy. Add the
banana, eggs, lemon zest, vanilla, baking
powder and spices. Run the machine
until thoroughly mixed, scraping the sides
as necessary.

Add the hazelnut meal, almond meal and
coconut. Process until well combined.

Spoon the batter into a large bowl and mix
the carrot and sultanas through.

193

Place paper cupcake cases inside the holes
of a 12-hole muffin tray. Spoon the batter
evenly into each case. Bake for 30–35
minutes until a skewer comes out clean
when inserted. Leave to cool completely
before topping.

Use an electric beater or a food processor
to whip together the topping ingredients.
Spread over each cake using a palate knife
or wide knife.

Store in the fridge in an airtight container for
up to four days.

BABY BANANA PIKELETS

We scoff these for breakfast, and if I make a double batch, I have them ready to go for lunchboxes or afternoon tea. Super simple and so handy. Try not to eat them all straight from the pan.

Makes 20 pikelets

194

1 very **ripe banana**
2 free-range **eggs** – lightly beaten
1 rounded teaspoon **honey / pure maple syrup**
1 teaspoon good-quality **vanilla essence**
¼ cup (30g) **tapioca flour**
¼ cup (35g) **brown rice flour**
Coconut oil / ghee (see page 198) for cooking

Combine all ingredients in a food processor or blender and run until the batter is smooth. Leave to sit for 10 minutes.

Heat a spoonful of oil in a sauté pan over a medium heat. For each pikelet, cook one tablespoon of batter until the surface is bubbly. Flip and cook for a further minute. You should be able to fit four pikelets in the pan at a time. Repeat until all the batter is used.

Pikelets can be stored in an airtight container for up to three days.

STAPLES

197

2 DF GF VEG NF GRFR

HOMEMADE MAYONNAISE

I'm a mayonnaise freak. I love the stuff. Especially with roasted vegetables or in a waldorf salad. I really don't like the nasty oils that store-bought varieties can be made with, so making mayonnaise from scratch is best. The process is incredibly simple. You'll be amazed (and pleased with yourself) when you see it come together in just a few minutes in the food processor. You can also mix it by hand – it'll just take a whole lot longer! Homemade mayo lasts for only eight days in the fridge so make a half batch if you don't think you will get through it all.

2 free-range **egg yolks**
1 tablespoon **apple cider vinegar**
Juice of ½ **lemon**
2 cups (500ml) **light olive oil**
1 teaspoon **sugar**
½ teaspoon **sea salt**

Place the egg yolks, vinegar and lemon juice in a food processor. With the machine running as slowly as possible start pouring the oil VERY slowly. About half way through you'll see it thicken and take on the consistency of mayonnaise. Continue pouring slowly. Turn off the food processor when all the oil is mixed in. Add the sugar and salt and mix for a further 5–10 seconds to combine.

Store in a glass jar in the fridge for up to eight days.

198

GF VEG NF GRFR

GHEE

Ghee is my favourite fat to cook with. It has long been used as a cooking oil in India and is considered a healing and balancing food in Ayurvedic practices. I love the gentle, rich flavour and stability when cooking over a high heat. It's very simple and inexpensive to make your own.

Typically you start with an unsalted butter. Truthfully, I've made this with salted butter plenty of times too. The salt sinks with the milk solids and is strained out.

Butter (I always use at least 500g at a time)

Put the butter in a large saucepan and place over a medium or low heat. It will melt and then start to bubble. Gently simmer for 25–40 minutes. Do not stir at any time during the process. You'll know the ghee is ready when the milk solids have sunk (they'll look lightly toasted) and you can see right to the bottom.

Leave to sit for 10 minutes before straining into a clean glass jar using a fine mesh strainer or cheesecloth.

GF (V) VEG NF GRFR

HOMEMADE YOGHURT

There are many reasons to embrace making your own yoghurt. It's so
simple and cheap, and most importantly, you'll know the good (gut-loving)
bacteria are still present because it's so fresh. A cheap milk thermometer
from a kitchen store, such as a home barista would use, will make it easy
to tell when the milk reaches the right temperature. I make my yoghurt in the
evening and by the morning it's all ready.

Makes 600ml

600ml **full-fat dairy milk**
2 rounded tablespoons of **yoghurt** from a
previous batch or store-bought yoghurt with
live cultures (check the label to ensure live
cultures are present)

Place the milk in a medium saucepan over a
high heat. Bring up to 90°C (195°F). Remove
from the heat and wait (about 10 minutes)
until the milk temperature has dropped to
40°C (105°F). Whisk in the yoghurt. Pour
into a large glass jar and put the lid on.
Wrap in a towel and place in the hot water
cupboard overnight. Alternatively use a
yoghurt maker to keep the yoghurt warm
for 10–16 hours. The longer you leave the
yoghurt fermenting the more lactose will be
consumed by the good bacteria. It will also
give a tarter end result.

To create thicker Greek-style yoghurt: Pour
yoghurt into a sieve lined with cheesecloth
(over a large bowl) and leave the whey to
drain out for 4–6 hours until the desired
thickness is achieved.

NUT BUTTER

Making homemade nut butter can save you a lot of money, as store-bought varieties can be expensive. I've been making my own for a long time. I'm lucky to now have a powerful high-speed blender that can do it in just a few minutes, although I made it for years in my regular (non-fancy) food processor. It requires a little patience but the end result is beautiful. You'll be high-fiving yourself when you make that first batch. Homemade nut butter also makes a great gift.

202

3 cups (420g) **raw nuts** – I most often use almonds or a cup each of almond, Brazil and cashew nuts
Salt to taste

Preheat oven to 150°C (300°F).

Spread nuts out evenly on a large ovenproof tray. Roast for 15–20 minutes. Set aside to cool for 10 minutes. Place the nuts in a food processor and start to run the machine. Process the nuts for 10–20 minutes (depending on the machine), until the nut butter is absolutely smooth and creamy. You will need to take lots of breaks within this time to both to scrape the sides of the food processor bowl and to prevent the motor overheating. The stages of making nut butter will appear as follows:

1. whole nuts
2. fine crumbs
3. sticky and solid mass
4. very coarse paste
5. smooth and creamy.

DO NOT add any extra oil or other liquid. It is not needed. Perseverance is key. The nuts will release their own oils (given enough time) to make perfectly smooth nut butter. Add salt to taste at the end.

SAUERKRAUT

Through the magic of fermentation, cabbage and salt are transformed into addictively tasty and oh-so-good-for-you sauerkraut. The good bacteria in sauerkraut nourish and promote a healthy gut environment.

Don't be intimidated by this basic fermentation. It's very simple and I've been making it for years without ever experiencing a batch go bad or mouldy. As long as you keep the cabbage submerged in the liquid you'll have success.

I love sauerkraut paired with cheese, meats and avocado. Honestly though, I'll find a way to incorporate it into most meals!

Makes enough to fill two to three 400ml jars

½ medium (450g) **green cabbage** – remove the outer leaves
½ medium (450g) **red cabbage** – remove the outer leaves
5 teaspoons **non-iodised salt** (iodine inhibits the necessary bacteria)
2–3 clean **jars** – wash beforehand with very hot soapy water and leave to air dry
Large **bowl** (or bucket) for mixing

Cut the cabbage into quarters and slice very thinly using a sharp knife or a mandolin. Place in the large bowl and sprinkle with salt – toss to disperse.

Using your (clean) hands, massage the cabbage vigorously for 5–10 minutes until it has softened, darkened and released lots of liquid. The longer you massage, the easier it is to pack into the jar.

Pack the softened cabbage and liquid VERY tightly into the jars leaving 2cm of air at the top (the cabbage will expand a little as the fermentation happens). The massinging process should leave you with plenty of liquid to fully submerge the cabbage in when pushed down tightly. Fermentation is an anaerobic activity (without oxygen) so it's important the cabbage comes in contact with as little air as possible and remains beneath the liquid to avoid contamination.

Place the jar lids on lightly and leave in a cool, dark place. A cupboard or pantry is ideal.

Check the sauerkraut every day during that first week. Use a clean fork to keep the cabbage pushed firmly under the liquid. After a few days it should get bubbly. After a few more days it will start to smell and taste sour. At the 10-day mark start tasting it. Once you are happy with the flavour place it in the fridge and enjoy.

I typically ferment my sauerkraut for 14–20 days. The process takes longer in winter and is much faster in summer. The thickness of the cabbage slices also affects the length of time it takes to ferment.

205

CAULIFLOWER (OR BROCCOLI) 'RICE'

Both cauliflower and broccoli make the most incredible rice substitute. You can serve it alongside your favourite curries, use it to make low-carb fried rice or as a tasty base to any nutritious meal. The key for me is to hit it with some good heat in the pan first to create good flavour.

206

½ head **cauliflower** / 2 heads **broccoli**
3 tablespoons **ghee** (see page 198)
or **coconut oil** for sautéing
Salt and **cracked black pepper**

Cut the cauliflower or broccoli into florets. Place in a food processor in 2–3 batches (it may not be able to chop evenly otherwise). Process until you achieve a rice-like consistency. Be careful not to blitz for too long, otherwise you'll end up with a fine mixture that will be mushy when cooked.

Heat a generous glug of ghee or coconut oil in a sauté pan over a high heat. Add the 'rice' and leave to sit for a moment to brown slightly. Move it around the pan for the next 3–5 minutes. Season generously with salt and pepper. Ideally serve immediately, but this 'rice' can also be reheated over a medium heat in a sauté pan.

Leftovers will keep in an airtight container in the fridge for up to two days.

CRUNCHY SEED CRACKERS

These crunchy delights are incredibly useful to have on hand. Partner with hummus, cheese, pickles, sliced avocado or sliced tomato for an easy snack. Enjoy them with either of my pâté recipes (see page 78 and 84) or crumble over hot soup.

Makes 20-25 crackers

1 ¼ cup (175g) **sunflower seeds**
⅓ cup (55g) **chia seeds**
(black or white are both fine)
¼ cup (40g) **sesame seeds**
½ teaspoon **sea salt**
1 teaspoon **fennel seeds** (optional)
2 tablespoons **melted coconut oil / olive oil**
3 tablespoons **water**
Cracked black pepper

Preheat oven to 180°C (350°F).

Place dry ingredients into a food processor and blitz for 2–3 minutes until the texture of coarse flour. Add the water and oil. Process until thoroughly mixed and sticky.

Form a rough ball and place on a large board or kitchen counter lined with baking paper. Place another piece of baking paper on top and roll out to around 1mm thick. Score the crackers with a knife both horizontally and vertically. Bake for 20–25 minutes in total until lightly golden. The outer crackers will cook first. I remove these (place on a wire rack to cool), and spread the remaining crackers out to help them cook on all edges. I'll do this 1–2 times throughout the cooking process. All crackers should be cooked after 25 minutes. Cool on a wire rack.

Crackers can be stored in an airtight container for up to five days.

Will freeze for up to one month (will soften slightly).

PESTO

Pesto is such a delicious (and often overlooked) way to eat a whole lot of greens. There really is no limit to the delicious combinations of nuts and fresh herbs that can be enjoyed year round. The following are some of my favourites but feel free to use these as inspiration for your own creations.

Generous seasoning really helps the pesto to shine.

210

Kale & walnut pesto

6 large **kale leaves**
½ cup (50g) **walnuts**
½ cup (60g) finely grated **parmesan**
½ small clove **garlic** – finely diced
Zest of 1 **lemon**
½ cup (125ml) **olive oil**
Salt and **cracked black pepper**

Blanch the kale leaves for 1 minute in boiling water before plunging into icy-cold water to halt the cooking and help retain the bright colour. Squeeze tightly to remove as much water as possible. Add to the food processor with the other ingredients. Blitz until the desired consistency.

Pistachio, mint & basil pesto (dairy-free)

½ cup (70g) **pistachio nuts**
½ cup (15g) **fresh mint leaves** – tightly packed
½ cup (15g) **fresh basil leaves** – tightly packed
½ small clove **garlic** – finely diced
½ cup (125ml) **olive oil**
Salt and **cracked black pepper**

Simply place all the pesto ingredients into a food processor and blitz until the desired consistency.

211

Parsley & cashew pesto

½ cup (70g) toasted **cashew nuts**
1 cup (25g) fresh **parsley leaves** – tightly packed
8 **capers**
Juice of 1 **lemon**
¼ cup (30g) finely grated **parmesan**
Salt and **cracked black pepper**

Simply place all the pesto ingredients into a food processor and blitz until the desired consistency.

Preparing your grain

These are the three grains I cook most often at home. In an ideal world you would always soak your grains before cooking. This helps remove their coating of phytic acid. Phytic acid binds to minerals, and means the goodness of the grain and the rest of the food you are enjoying it with is not assimilated as well as it could be. Busy lives means it's not always possible to pre-soak. There are certainly days when I don't manage to do this. Squeezing in even an hour of soaking will help.

Simply cover the grain with cold water in a large bowl. You can use plain water or add a couple of teaspoons of lemon juice or apple cider vinegar to help the soaking process. Leave for 8–12 hours. Drain and rinse well.

MILLET

Hulled millet is my favourite gluten-free grain. When cooked, it is deliciously fluffy and nutritious – rich in B vitamins and iron. I prefer to cook it in stock as it absorbs the flavour beautifully but you can just use water. It's much less expensive than quinoa, making it a great everyday option. If I'm feeling like a bit of extra richness (which is often) I stir through a big spoonful of butter before serving.

1 cup (180g) **hulled millet**
2 cups **vegetable / chicken stock**
1 **bay leaf** (optional)

Place the millet, stock and bay leaf in a medium saucepan and bring to the boil. Reduce to a simmer and cook for around 15 minutes with the lid slightly ajar, until the millet is tender and the liquid has been absorbed. Discard the bay leaf.

QUINOA

Quinoa has been a health food hero of late and with legitimate reason. It's a source of plant-based protein, fibre and essential amino acids. White quinoa is the most common variety available, but do try to get your hands on the red or black variety. I love the pop of colour they add to your plate. All three varieties require the same method of cooking.

Quinoa can have a grassy flavour that some people do not like. I find soaking the grain beforehand in a large bowl of cold water for at least a few hours, or rinsing VERY well, eliminates a lot of this.

Cooking quinoa in stock rather than water will add a lovely flavour but is not essential. Cooking in a 50/50 mixture of water and coconut milk is also great when pairing with Asian dishes.

1 cup (200g) **quinoa**
2 cups (500ml) **water**
or **chicken / vegetable stock**

Rinse the quinoa well under running water if you haven't soaked the grains. I like to use my hand to swish the grains around in the water and then drain in a fine sieve. The quinoa water will run clear when it's well washed – usually after four rinses.

Bring the quinoa and cooking water or stock to the boil. Reduce to a simmer and cook for 12–15 minutes with the lid slightly ajar until tender and the liquid has been absorbed. Place the lid on fully and leave to sit for 5 minutes before fluffing with a fork.

213

BROWN RICE

I enjoy the firm bite and chewiness of brown rice. It really benefits from soaking. This will speed up the cooking time and give it a pleasant tenderness. Soak for 8–12 hours for the best results. Rinse well and cook as normal.

1 cup (190g) **brown rice**
2 cups (500ml) **water**

Bring brown rice and water to the boil in a saucepan. Reduce to a simmer and cook for 45 minutes, with the lid slightly ajar, until tender and the liquid has been absorbed.

BONE BROTH

I make bone broth most weeks in my kitchen. I love having a good supply of it on hand at all times. An incredibly nutrient-dense and healing food, it's loaded with collagen and glycine to look after your gut health and strengthen skin, hair, nails and your immune system. Its goodness is easy to digest, making it an effective elixir. It's quite amazing that such a simple food can serve your body so well. I urge anyone who is interested in moving to a more wholefoods diet to start by introducing homemade bone broth. It's both cheap AND simple to prepare.

You can use the broth in soups, simmer it down to make jus, add to Bolognese sauce and other braises, or simply drink by the mugful with a generous seasoning of salt and pepper.

When sourcing bones, there are two options. Either use those from meal leftovers or source them from your local butcher. For the former, a roast chicken carcass is the most obvious, but I also collect smaller bones like leftovers from lamb shoulder or neck chops, chicken wings or drumsticks. Simply store in the freezer – a zip-lock bag is ideal – until you have enough to make stock.

If you have sourced raw bones from your local butcher it can be a good idea to roast these beforehand to add more flavour to the finished broth. Preheat your oven to 180°C (350°F) and roast for 25 minutes or until well browned.

Flavour your stock with the combination of vegetables I have prescribed on the following page or collect vegetable scraps from your meal preparation and store these in the freezer until you're ready to make broth. The best choices are onions, carrot, celery, zucchini, green beans and leeks. It's best to avoid broccoli, cauliflower and beetroot as they are either too strong in flavour or will colour your stock (in the case of beetroot).

Place the bones, vegetables, herbs and water in a very large pot. Add the cider vinegar. Bring to a boil. Reduce to simmer and cook for 4–8 hours. Skim any brown foam from the top periodically. Alternatively you can bring to a boil and then pour into a slow cooker to cook on low for two days.

Strain broth through a fine sieve and set aside to cool for 20 minutes before decanting into clean jars.

1kg **bones** / 1 **chicken carcass**
(aim to have some marrow bones in there if
making beef or lamb broth)
3 cups (approximately) **vegetable scraps**
(can also use 1 **onion** – cut into quarters,
2 **carrots** – sliced, 3 stalks **celery** – cut to fit
into the pot, 4 cloves **garlic**)
4 tablespoons **apple cider vinegar**
8L **water**
1 **bay leaf** (optional)
Handful **parsley stalks** (optional)

Broth tips

If the smell of bone broth simmering in your kitchen is a little overpowering (beef bones can be quite strong), add parsley stalks every couple of hours. I find them really effective as an odour neutraliser.

Cooled bone broth will have a solid layer of cooled fat on top. You can simply remove and discard or be very waste-free and use it instead of your usual oil when sautéing.

Stock can be frozen for up to six months. Thawed stock should be used within 3– 4 days. Store at the back of the fridge, especially during summer.

Decant the stock into different-sized containers that best serves how you intend to use it. Freeze larger portions for soup and risotto and smaller amounts for adding to dishes such as Bolognese, or for additional flavour in rice dishes and for de-glazing the pan.

I find clean 400g peanut butter jars a great way to store stock. They fit perfectly in the door of my freezer. Just leave an inch of space at the top to allow for the liquid to expand.

215

217

220

THANK YOU

Thank you Beatnik Publishing, especially Sally and Kitki, for making this dream happen. I'm so excited to have made something beautiful together.

I owe a huge amount of thanks to my wonderful recipe testers for taking my recipes into their home kitchens and serving them up to flatmates and families. Your feedback was invaluable, Anna McArthur, Amy O'Malley, Ash Scott, Bonnie De Gros, Elizabeth Kriechbaum, Jane Barnett, Jemma Field, Katrina Tanner, Lisette Scholten, Louise Woolhouse, Mai Barton, Michaela Bratty, Tania Loveridge and Trinity Doyle.

A big thank you to Father Rabbit, Bianca Lorenne, Citta design, Bec Ploughman Cermaics and Sonia Nagels for the beautiful props.

Thank you Aimee Finlay Magne for being such a sweet soul to work with. Being photographed has never been so comfortable.

Thank you to Juliette Hogan and Miss Crabb for the gorgeous clothes to be photographed in.

Susan Williams, thank you for editing my final recipes, for always generously lending me your beautiful bits and pieces for styling, for patiently letting me talk your ear off about food and for inspiring me with your approach to gardening and cooking.

Arti Badiani, you took this dream seriously from day one and I won't ever forget that. Thank you dear friend.

My darling Luke. From the bottom of my heart, thank you for embarking on this food writing journey with me. Your hard work has anchored our little family and you've given me space to grow. I love you dearly.

My precious Bonnie, chief taster and kitchen apprentice. Your big heart and wild imagination inspire your mama more than you could ever know. I can't wait to co-write a book with you one day.

Mum and Dad, thank you for always letting your mad daughter follow her heart and being there to pick up the pieces when necessary. Your love has lifted me up.

223

Beatnik Publishing

PO Box 8276, Symonds Street,
Auckland 1150, New Zealand

www.beatnikpublishing.com